The Word Among Us

for Terry and Sharon,
who live by another ocean
but are near in spirit.

The Word Among Us

Reflections on the Readings of the Revised
Common Lectionary

Year C Volume 2

Herbert O'Driscoll

Anglican Book Centre
Toronto, Canada

1998
Anglican Book Centre
600 Jarvis Street
Toronto, Ontario
M4Y 2J6

Cover illustration: "The Three Marys and the Angel at Christ's Tomb," Nerius

Canadian Cataloguing in Publication Data

O'Driscoll, herbert, 1928-
    The word among us : reflections on the readings of the revised common lectionary

ISBN 1-55126-195-2 (Year C, v. 2)

1. Bible – Criticism, interpretation, etc. 2. Bible – Liturgical lessons, English. I. Title.

BS511.5.037 1997   220.7   C97-932166-2

Contents

Using This Book

Someone once said that preaching is much more the story of an eye operation as told by the person who has just been given back sight, than it is the story as told by the surgeon who has just done the operation.

This thought occurs to me because I am more and more certain that if the preacher is not committed personally to what he or she is saying, then something essential is missing from the moment. The other reason I tell it is that I have written these pages with what I hope is a certain intimacy and an overall personal style. I have constantly seen myself as being with the reader as we think together about the lessons of a Sunday.

Some readers may have used a previous series called *Child of Peace: Lord of Life*. This new series, on the readings of the Revised Common Lectionary, is in no way a revision of the former series. I have deliberately set aside the former books and have not referred to them in any way.

These pages are not ready-made homilies. They respect the fact that scripture, the sermon formed from it, the person giving the homily, and the congregation, all form a living entity in which wonderful things can happen. These pages may also be useful for those who wish to build a Bible study group around the lectionary readings, or for the individual worshipper who wishes to give the readings some thought before joining in worship.

A word about my treatment of the psalms. Very frequently only a portion of the psalm is used. In most instances I have offered a reflection on the psalm as a whole. I have done this in the hope that the reflections on the pslams might be useful in themselves as short talks for various occasions.

My hope is that these reflections will open some doors to homilies that will eventually turn out very differently from my notes! With this book go my prayers and best wishes for your part in the ministry of our Lord in which we both share.

Herbert O'Driscoll.
Advent 1997

First Sunday in Lent

Deuteronomy 26:1–11
Psalm 91:1–2, 9–16
Romans 10:8b–13
Luke 4:1–13

Weavings

In all circumstances of life, a strong faith in God can give direction and grace.

First Reading. Year after year the people of God bring to God the first fruits of the earth, acknowledging that these gifts are theirs only by God's grace.

The Psalm. To *live in the shelter of the Most High* — a beautiful expression for possessing the presence of God in one's life.

Second Reading. An assurance that our trust in God through Jesus Christ will save us from meaninglessness in life.

The Gospel. Our Lord, wrestling with decisions about different ways to carry out his vocation, places the will of God above all other considerations.

Note

Sometimes I find it helpful to scan a season's readings to see if there are continuing themes. The five gospels of Lent this year show us something about our Lord's ministry that many people may miss. This is the cost of his ministry, the cost to him as a human being.

We see very clearly the cost of his ministry in terms of suffering and death. I wonder sometimes if we give enough thought to the cost in terms of stress and tension. Let us look at the five passages in sequence.

Lent 1. The extended stress of deciding alone how he will act in the months and years ahead of him.

Lent 2. The constant pressure from powerful and dangerous people like Herod, and the unrelenting politics of dealing with established structures such as the Pharisees.

Lent 3. As we listen to Jesus correcting the thinking of the disciples, we perceive a vehemence in his words. I think I detect a sense of frustration and tension. The moment culminates in the very real sternness of the parable of the fig tree.

Lent 4. Only if we take note of the opening verses of the gospel for the Fourth Sunday, do we realize that this story of the two sons is highly political. Notice to whom it is told. On the one hand, there are tax collectors and sinners; on the other, Pharisees and scribes. The former would see themselves as the forgiven and welcomed younger son; the others, as the older son who knows nothing of forgiveness. There is ample cause for anger and resentment, resulting in real danger for Jesus.

Lent 5. The evening in the Bethany home is suddenly made an occasion of tension by Mary's sudden gesture. The snide remark of Judas is hurtful. The incident obviously reminds Jesus of the awful possibilities that lie ahead. A measure of his tension is the sharp correction aimed at Judas: *"Leave her alone!"*

Reflections

First Reading

The terms of the settlement are right up front. This is not just any land and any settlement. Life has not just brought them here by happenstance. This is *the land that the Lord your God is giving you as an inheritance to possess.*

One cannot help but notice the precision of this passage. The instructions are detailed and vivid. We can see people living and acting. They move on to the land and begin to till it. The first crop appears and is harvested. *You shall take some of the first of all the fruit.* Notice the emphasis on *the first* — this is not to be an afterthought after everything else is done!

You shall put it in a basket and go to the place that the Lord your God will choose as a dwelling for his name. One cannot but be intrigued by the idea of God choosing where the divine presence will dwell. We tend to build our churches and then assume that our choice of place is necessarily God's! One cannot help wondering where else God has chosen to dwell. Should we be continually open to the possibility of the Holy Being in all sorts of unexpected places?

Notice the phrase, *the land that the Lord your God is giving you.* We might expect the expression, *"has given you."* Instead, there is the implication that our relationship with God is one of *always* receiving. I am never in full possession of my life. Rather, I am always continuing to receive it. Far from suggesting that this makes me dependent, it gives me the good news that there is always more to be received, if I am prepared to remain open to receiving.

Even the words of this ritual are given in detail. You shall say this … the priest shall say … you shall reply … and so on. You shall say, *I declare to the Lord … that I have come into the land … A wandering Aramean was my ancestor … The Lord brought us out of Egypt … So now I bring the first of the fruit … that you, O Lord, have given me.* Why is this all spelled out so precisely? Because saying something — actually speaking the words — is extremely important. Naming is powerful. The world of the Bible knew this. In worship, we name things. This is why it is vitally important to worship. Above all, we name God. In confession, we name aspects of ourselves that need to be faced — and they can be faced if we name them. In praise, we name aspects of our faith that we would never dream of doing amid the daily business of our lives. In intercession, we name our concern, and even love, for other people. We name issues and needs that otherwise might never occur to us. In a sense, to name something is to bring it into existence in a new way. As in a ritual such as we have here, to name my dependence on God is to continually recreate and enrich my relationship with this God.

The Psalm

The opening lines are among the loveliest in the psalms. They seem to express perfectly a deep and abiding relationship be-tween God and my humanity. I instinctively find them forming into a personal prayer. "O God most high, shelter my life, that I, living in the shadow of your greatness, may always know you to be my fortress, my God in whom I trust." As one says this prayer, one can also hear the words of the hymn, "Be thou my vision."

Because you have made the Lord your refuge … no evil [shall] happen to you. Not for a moment can we take this as literally true for our lives. To do so would be to court spiritual disaster and to demean the truth about our relationship with

God. All the faith in the world cannot guarantee that we will not have to face what Shakespeare called "the slings and arrows of outrageous fortune." We have only to look about us at people whom we know most certainly to have a deep and genuine faith in God, whom we have visited and befriended and cared for as they went through great suffering. The psalmist had only to look around to see evidence on every side that the most genuine faith cannot ward off dreadful things.

How then are we to read these lines? The psalmist speaks of God commanding his angels *to keep you in all your ways.* We hear God say, *Those who love me, I will deliver ... I will be with them in trouble.* This last phrase helps us to understand what the psalmist is saying. He is obviously not denying that there will be trouble in life. He is not saying that Christian faith can give us a kind of teflon layer that protects us from everything. But we are being told that God will be with us: *I will be with them in trouble. I will rescue them and honour them.* In other words, Christian faith is not a protection against trouble, but it can be a rich spiritual resource when trouble comes.

Second Reading

The word is ... on your lips and in your heart (that is, the word of faith that we proclaim). Notice here how Paul speaks of the word that is not only in our hearts but also on our lips. Again, we are back to the need for us to name the faith that is in us, to speak of it. Notice that Paul doesn't just refer to "the word of faith" but *the word of faith that we proclaim.* He is almost saying that faith is not fully faith until it is in some way proclaimed.

Today Christians are in a new relationship with the society around them. Christian faith is now a personally chosen faith. Society places no sanctions on those who do not believe it. It follows that Christians must discover viable ways in which to speak of their faith when the moment and the situation make this possible and desirable. For so long has this element of proclamation been absent from our Christian experience, that it will probably take more than a generation for full awareness of the new reality to dawn.

If you confess with your lips ... and believe in your heart. We have tended to emphasize the need for believing the faith in our hearts, at the expense of speaking it with our lips. Here we are being told that we need to do both. There is a time for naming Christian faith. There are certainly clumsy and intrusive ways to do this, and we hear them from time to time. We need to find ways of witnessing to Christian faith that are true to who and what we are. There are many quiet moments, with a friend or with a colleague at work, when we talk about the stresses on our lives, personal and professional. Think how effective it can be when someone in a conversation says quite naturally that he or she finds immense strength and encouragement in the life of a certain Christian community, and then issues a non-threatening invitation to that life.

No less than three times in this short passage, Paul uses the term "saved." *If you confess ... Jesus ... you will be saved. One confesses ... and so is saved ... Everyone who calls on the name of the Lord shall be saved.* How can we hear this language today? What is it that I am to be saved from? Perhaps it is best to answer this question personally. Doing this releases each one of us to seek our own words.

I find in myself a deep conviction that I am not self-sufficient. Much is lacking in me. In the language of Christian faith, I am conscious of being a "sinner." Having been brought up a Christian, I am aware that my humanity has, in Jesus Christ, been lived with a beauty and perfection so far beyond mine as to constitute not only a difference of degree but a difference in kind. I bow myself before this living out of my humanity in Jesus. For this reason I call him Lord.

I am aware also that he was prepared to encounter the darkness of human nature that exists in myself, in all others, and in all human institutions — challenging this darkness even to the point of a dreadful death. I am aware that this death was not capable of extinguishing the light and glory of his presence. In the utterly simple yet incomparably profound language of Christian faith, I believe that on the third day he rose from the dead, and will come to judge the living and the dead, among whom I shall be.

I find that to believe these things, and in this clumsy and groping way to "confess" them, saves me from many things. It saves me from seeing my single short life as without meaning — which is to be spared a tragically common contemporary disease. It saves me from thinking of myself as self-sufficient, or from having to try desperately to become self-sufficient. It saves me from carrying endless guilt about the pathetic (perhaps I should use the older word "miserable") elements of my thoughts and actions. Again, in the timeless language of the faith, it saves me from being overcome by my own "sin." It deals with this sin, not by excusing it or denying it, but by forgiving it! For which I wish to say, thanks be to God!

The Gospel

When at various stages of life, we find ourselves in a "wilderness situation" — a time of confusion, fear, anxiety, doubt — it can be immensely encouraging to notice eight simple words at the beginning of this gospel passage, words that we might easily miss if we read too quickly. It is the statement, *Jesus ... was led by the Spirit in the wilderness.*

These words can be encouraging for us because they tell us two things about the way God sometimes deals with us. If our Lord was *led by the Spirit* at this juncture, it tells us that our periods of wilderness can be occasions for the leading of God's

Holy Spirit, and may even have been given to us for this purpose. The statement can be encouraging in another way. It suggests that the Holy Spirit is already in the wilderness before we even get there!

For forty days he was tempted by the devil. At first reading, this sentence seems far removed from our lives. Yet, in the language of the Bible, we are being told that not every problem in our lives can be solved quickly and easily. There may be times when we have to bow our heads, face the possibility of a long haul, and plod through, reaching for all the resources we can find. The biblical *forty days* means simply, a long time. *Tempted by the devil* may not, in our day, call up pictures of being harassed by a large dark figure with horns and cloven feet! This does not mean, however, that you and I have not often met the demons encountered by Jesus at this period in his life.

Notice, for instance, the way that the demon repeats the phrase, *If you are the Son of God.* Perhaps we should hear it said sneeringly. We may be seeing our Lord wrestle with something we know very well — self-doubt. Who am I? Am I really the person who I think and hope I am? Can I be what I think I am being called to be? We have all heard these voices whispering in our ear.

Notice also something that all the temptations have in common. All appeal to the ego as being self-sufficient. In every case the demon is saying, "You can do this. You can be this." *Command this stone to become a loaf of bread.* We are hearing the temptation to attract followers through bribery, by producing what they want and need. Our Lord refuses.

The devil showed him ... all the kingdoms of the world. The temptation is to get people to follow by the use of naked power. If you don't want to bribe them, then dominate them. Again our Lord refuses.

Throw yourself down from the pinnacle of the temple. The third option the demon offers is the possibility of impressing people so much that they will be mesmerized by spectacle and will follow. Jesus once again refuses.

Notice the basis on which Jesus always refuses. Every option is an appeal to his human ego, and for every option, Jesus points to a reference beyond himself. He defers to a will higher than his own — God's will for his life and ministry. *Worship the Lord your God, and serve only him ... Do not put the Lord your God to the test.* Some time in the future, Jesus will kneel in Gethsemane and actually say to God, *Not my will but thine be done.* It is easy to miss the fact that this is precisely what he is saying here in the wilderness in an implicit way.

Incidentally, what does Jesus choose to do when he has refused the methods of the demon? He returns to Galilee, walks down the shoreline of the lake, and calls his first two disciples. He has chosen not the way of the solitary ego, but the way of community, sharing, relationship.

Luke ends this passage with a line that is haunting, and that expresses a universal truth about all our lives. *When the devil had finished every test, he departed from him until an opportune time.* The demon does not depart permanently, even from Jesus. There will be other encounters, other struggles. We know only too well that this is true for our lives. But we know something else — because of the risen life of our Lord, there is grace for us in our encounters with the demon.

Second Sunday in Lent

Genesis 15:1–12, 17–18
Psalm 27
Philippians 3:17–4:1
Luke 13:31–35

Weavings

In each of the first readings there is a sense of something threatening that must be faced.

First Reading. Abram has to wrestle with his own inner doubts about the future course of his life.

The Psalm. There is a sense of fear. Enemies threaten the psalmist, and he seeks the help of God.

Second Reading. Writing to the community at Philippi, Paul warns against those who may be enemies of the new faith.

The Gospel. Some Pharisees come to Jesus and warn him that he is in danger from Herod's plotting against him.

Reflections

First Reading

As an example of the Bible's readiness to be honest about its heroic figures, this passage is classic. Here we see Abram, the seemingly towering founding figure of a future people, nervous and insecure! We hear the voice of God making effort to reassure Abram. *Do not be afraid, Abram, I am your shield; your reward shall be very great.* The words could be said to a fearful child and not be out of place. Interestingly, they do not have the slightest effect in calming Abram's fears. Yet this is the person who has come down in history as the wonderful example of a person who trusts God!

Abram's real agenda appears immediately. *O Lord God, what will you give me, for I continue childless?* In his desperation, he repeats the complaint. *You have given me no offspring.* God tries again to reassure, using the language of a patient but loving adult dealing with a child. *No one but your very own issue shall be your heir.*

It seems that even this is not enough. The child in Abram will not be comforted by words. Something else is needed. Abram stands under the dome of the desert sky at night. Only in such a place can the true glory of the stars be seen. The Lord says, *Look toward heaven and count the stars, if you are able to count them.* Abram gazes upward. The majesty of the night sky has a calming effect on his worries about the future. *So shall your descendants be.* For a moment, Abram is reassured. *He believed the Lord.* God continues to bolster Abram's still fragile trust. *I am the Lord who brought you from Ur of the Chaldeans.* It would seem that God is appealing to Abram's past confidence in his own decisions and actions. Perhaps God suggests that the younger Abram would not have behaved like this. This episode may be reminding us how advancing years can rob us of our earlier easy certainties about our ability to handle our lives.

Once again reassurance fails. It is not enough for Abram to hear that God had promised him this land. Instead, there is a desperate request for guarantees. *O Lord God, how am I to know that I shall possess it?*

There is no direct response, perhaps because it is simply not given to us to know the future in the way that Abram — and each of us — wants so very much to know. From what we can see here, God moves Abram beyond words, beyond arguments, beyond his fevered efforts to think the problem through. Abram moves into ritual, into acting out his fears, offering them to the God from whom he cannot wrest the certainties our fearful humanity longs for. He lays out the sacrifice. *A heifer ... a female goat ... a ram ... a turtledove ... a young pigeon.* Birds of prey swoop down, symbolic of Abram's own dark brooding doubts and fears. The scarlet fire of the desert sun dies away. Darkness sweeps over Abram, taking him into a troubled sleep. *A deep and terrifying darkness descended upon him.*

There are some inner voices that cannot be quieted by words of comfort, some demons that will not go away until we have allowed them to work their will on us. Fear, guilt, anxiety, depression, sorrow. We encounter them at different times in our journey through tracts of desert. As with Abram, we will receive grace from God, but we must still wrestle with the demons. The grace does not banish the demons. It merely gives us sufficient strength to battle them. And at the end of the day, we sleep, sometimes like Abram encountering *deep and terrifying darkness,* but always rising again to a new day and to further journeying.

The Psalm

As in the previous reading we are hearing a very honest portrayal of the human nature we all share. In a sense, it is a shout of unassailable confidence: *The Lord is my light ... The Lord is the strength of my life; of whom shall I be afraid?* But it is also an implicit admission that we express this confidence precisely because we also experience a frequent sense of great vulnerability. *When evildoers came upon me to eat up my flesh ... Though an army [should] encamp against me.* There is no denying that life can bring its moments of fear and threat.

One thing I have asked ... [to] dwell in the house of the Lord ... [that he will] keep me safe in his shelter ... hide me in the secrecy of his dwelling. Freud frequently dismissed religious faith as nothing more than a crutch, a pathetic compensation for our fearful humanity. While Christian faith would deny the truth of this accusation, we have to acknowledge that human nature does need some sense of there being a place of refuge, an ally, a source of grace beyond the self, as we seek to deal with the experiences of life.

As we read further, we realize that the psalmist is asking for something much deeper and stronger than an imaginary faceless power looming behind our human efforts. This help will be real — not like a cartoon superman figure whom we call to our aid when all efforts fail. What is being spoken of here is a relationship. *You speak in my heart and say, "Seek my face." Your face, Lord, will I seek.* What is being sought is a continuing and deepening relationship. *Teach me your way, O Lord ... lead me on a level path because of my enemies.*

All the time in these verses there is an obvious realism about life. Enemies, whether external or internal, are always to be encountered. We are not asking for a God who demolishes our enemies. We seek a relationship with a God who stands with us as we face them. *Be strong, and he shall comfort your heart; wait patiently for the Lord.*

Second Reading

Judging from the tone of this letter to the Christian community in Philippi, things have gone very well since its inception. There is as yet no sign of the divisive forces that were so common in other communities. Paul is almost euphoric in the way he addresses them. *My brothers and sisters, whom I love and long for, my joy and crown … my beloved.*

Yet even here, Paul sees danger. There will in time — there may already be — very different role models, among whom they will have to make choices. *Observe those who live according to the example you have in us. For many live as enemies of the cross of Christ.* Left like this, the question is wide open as to whom or to what Paul is referring. But he continues, *Their god is the belly; and their glory is in their shame.*

We need to know a little about the kind of society that Christian faith was coming to birth in. By this time, the Roman Empire was a vast, immensely varied, and mature society. It had been in existence a long time. It was beginning to show signs of the more marked decadence that would come later and contribute to its demise. The old disciplines were beginning to slip, and cynicism was creeping into attitudes. Many were developing an excessive craving for the satisfaction of human appetites, whether for rich and exotic foods, for ways of pampering the body, or for endless sexual possibilities. There were many more critical voices than that of Paul — not necessarily all Christian — who expressed regret and gave warning.

But Paul is among the critics in moments such as this. He hints at many meanings when he speaks of *the body of our humiliation.* He maintains that this body, with all its appetites, constantly seeks and needs transformation. Paul is not expressing a hatred of the body, merely a clear-eyed knowledge that the body can become a tyrant in its demands, especially during periods of great change. Fears and anxieties and insecurities can trigger many neurotic responses, such as alcoholism, food addictions, and a restless and demanding sexuality. Those who possess in their lives sources of liberating hope, ideals that call for fulfillment — what many would call a higher purpose — have some means of resisting such temptations.

We are expecting a Saviour. For Paul and the Christians of Philippi, as for Christians today, the ultimate source of hope and the ultimate ideal is our Lord Jesus Christ. And *our citizenship ... in heaven* — the Christian vision of the Holy City — can be the pattern for our citizenship here in time and history.

The Gospel

Pharisees came and said to him, "Get away from here, for Herod wants to kill you." The Pharisees get such a poor press in the gospels that it is almost startling to hear them advising Jesus about a threat from Herod. Yet this incident is a reminder to us that much of the New Testament dislike of the Pharisees may derive from the early Christian communities at the time of writing, and not so much from Jesus' own time. It is obvious that our Lord's relationship with the these people was not ideal, but moments like this suggest that the reality was more complex than we have been led to believe. Pharisees can undoubtedly be as much the victim of stereotyping as anyone else!

Our Lord's reply is fascinating, if only for its tone. By telling what is said and how it is said, this passage reveals a facet of Jesus' personality. It also reveals a mood. *Go and tell that fox for me ...* is full of intense dislike, even contempt. This imprecation is immediately followed by a terse statement of what he is doing. It is hurled as a direct challenge: *Listen, I am casting out demons and performing cures today and tomorrow.* Perhaps Jesus realizes that there may not be much time left to him. There is in the phrase *on the third day I finish my work* an authority that is almost majestic. The implication is that nothing can stop the completion of what Jesus is about, not even death itself. This note of defiance is continued in the words, *Today, tomorrow, and the next day I must be on my way.* This work will continue despite all the Herods in the world. Then the note of heavy sarcasm returns, *because it is impossible for a prophet to be killed outside of Jerusalem.* An oblique way of saying it is highly likely that any prophet who dares to challenge his society in Jerusalem will indeed be killed.

Now there is an abrupt change of tone, as if Jesus is overcome by the tragedy of it all. Many voices have called this great city of Jerusalem to the way of God, and many have been rejected, some even killed. This may be one of those moments when Jesus realizes that his mission may exact the highest and most terrible of costs.

This may be one of those times when we are allowed into the humanity of our Lord. We share his deepest feelings at a time of tension and even fear. There may also be a deep sense of loneliness at this juncture. While we all know that there are those who dislike us (in professional life there may even be those who wish us ill), it can be particularly dispiriting and chilling to have the actual sources of aversion or threat specifically identified. When this sort of experience comes to us, we can be strengthened by knowing that our Lord was no stranger to such intimidation and even attack, and that he met it with courage and determination. As with any passage of the gospel, this interpretation by no means exhausts the possible meanings, but merely suggests one way in which we can approach it.

Third Sunday in Lent

Isaiah 55:1–9
Psalm 63:1–8
1 Corinthians 10:1–13
Luke 13:1–9

Weavings

To be human is to long for many things. Those who long after God will find themselves satisfied. They will also find a God in whom judgement and mercy are mingled together.

First Reading. Isaiah encourages his people to refrain from seeking anything less than God, the ultimately satisfying source of satisfaction.

The Psalm. A song in which the whole mind and heart of the singer is focused on God.

Second Reading. Paul reminds the new Christian community in Corinth that an earlier people of God became so enamoured of the things of the self that they forgot God.

The Gospel. Jesus reminds those listening to him that life is a gift of God, and our use of it will be judged by the degree to which we return it in service to God.

Reflections

First Reading

A passionate plea that rings down the ages. *Why do you spend your money for that which is not bread?* Isaiah is pleading for a renewed set of values in his society. Notice that he fully acknowledges certain realities. There are those *that have no money.* But even they can find something to make a difference in their lives. There is sustenance to satisfy a thirst. There is a certain *wine and milk* that does not cost money, a certain kind of *rich food.*

Isaiah is not indulging in a version of Marie Antoinette's response to being told that the poor were hungry. Her famous, or infamous, reply was, "Let them eat cake." Neither is Isaiah offering "pie in the sky when you die." If he were, this passage would confirm Marx's slur that religion is the opium of the people.

I will make with you an everlasting covenant ... Nations that do not know you shall run to you. Remember that Isaiah is addressing his society as a whole. When he speaks of God offering this people a covenant, we know that he, like all the prophets, is seeing any such covenant as extending through all society. God covenanting with the whole people of God meant that every part of the people covenanted with every other part, and the criteria of covenant in the Bible is always justice. In Isaiah's great vision, other nations will run to Israel because it shines among the nations as a society of justice. The quality of the nation's life will make it *a witness to the peoples, a leader and commander for the peoples.*

Isaiah is not calling for a new kind of spirituality that ignores the realities of the world around it. The renewal he is demanding will have real consequences in thinking and action.

Let the wicked forsake their way, and the unrighteous their thoughts. Among such concrete results would be the forming of a society of justice where those who need bread will have it!

The genius of Judaism has always been to root all religious experience in reality. It is never enough to be merely other worldly. It is absolutely essential to have spiritual goals, but never without an eye to the necessary repercussions in this world. The old Jewish tag speaks of "praying as if everything depended on God and acting as if everything depended on oneself."

This passage speaks eloquently to much that is happening in our own society. Since, in recent years, great changes in social thinking and planning have taken place, it is paramount that the consequences of those changes are examined in terms of this vision of Isaiah. There are two issues, stated here broadly.

First, what are the values and moral standards of the kind of society we are building? In itself, wealth is neither good nor bad, but we need to guard against the danger of the accumulation of wealth becoming the primary purpose of life. There is already much evidence that such a limited goal has sad effects on human personality and relationships. How does a society such as ours guard against the imbalances that develop within it — the presence of those who, for genuine reasons, fall between the cracks of the new affluence and are therefore truly needy? In Isaiah's terms, what covenant must we form in our society to sustain its fundamental health? One thing is certain: if a society is not morally healthy, it will eventually disintegrate.

Second, how is meaning to be found in contemporary life? Again, to use Isaiah's terms, what thoughts and ideas must a society reach for beyond its own instinctively acquisitive thinking? We hear this in the magnificent words that Isaiah puts into the mouth of God: *My thoughts are not your thoughts ... My ways [are] higher than your ways and my thoughts than your thoughts.*

The Psalm

As is so frequent in the psalms, we are in the area of the deeply personal. We are, in effect, overhearing a person who has moved into the presence of God and is expressing the depth of feeling and thought that comes in such moments. *You are my God, eagerly I seek you; my soul thirsts for you.* The language is almost startlingly that of a lover. There is even a physical element in the language. *My flesh faints for you.* Then comes the simile that echoes the language of Isaiah in the previous passage: *As in a barren and dry land where there is no water.*

The use of the term "weary" reminds us of the fondness that Victorian hymn writers had for describing this world as weary — sometimes also dreary! We need to remember that this proclivity is not biblical. The Bible does not try to overwhelm us with a weary and dreary world. The Bible is much more given to portraying the world as a shining and vibrant creation of God. It becomes a place where we can consider "weary" only in the absence of God! The irony is that, to some degree, our perception is our own choice.

So that we can avoid finding ourselves in *a barren and dry land where there is no water,* we need to consider what we see the psalmist doing. *I have gazed upon you in your holy place.* In other words, I have gone to places of worship. *[Beholding your power and glory.]* I deliberately meditate on the ways that the glory of God can appear in my experience. *My mouth praises you with joyful lips.* I have actually expressed my praise for God. *I ... meditate on you in the night watches.* Even when my humanity is most vulnerable — perhaps, particularly when it is so — I try to concentrate my thoughts on God as my source of strength and hope. *My soul clings to you.* I readily acknowledge my dependence as a creature. *Your right hand holds me fast.* I joyfully reach out for a strength beyond my own.

Second Reading

This letter to Corinth was obviously difficult for Paul to write. It involved disciplining a wayward community — even being harsh. We can be quite sure that Paul did not enjoy this job any more than anybody else would, but he was prepared to do it. This is worth noting because of the mistaken conviction among many in today's church that somehow it is less than Christian to confront problematical issues in the life of the community.

At this stage Paul reminds his listeners of a salutary incident in Jewish history. He can confidently do so because, for many in the new Christian community, this history was their own. Notice the many times he uses the word "all." *Our ancestors were all under the cloud, and all passed through the sea, and all were baptized ... and all ate the same spiritual food, and all drank the same spiritual drink.* I suspect Paul wishes to emphasize that, through thick or thin, the people of God stayed together. He may be doing this because the people in Corinth — as in many congregations today — were tending all too easily to accept divisions and alienations, instead of regarding the unity of God's people as the primary concern, to be sought by every effort.

Notice the reason Paul gives for the people of God staying together. *They drank from the spiritual rock that followed them, and the rock was Christ.* Paul is saying that our Lord acts as the rock for any Christian community. If the community keeps our Lord as the prime focus of its life and work, then he will also be its source of unity.

But here we see the absolute realism of Paul. Communities are made up of all too human men and women — people like ourselves! Things happen. Things go wrong. In that long-ago wilderness — even long-ago for those to whom Paul was writing — things went very wrong. *God was not pleased with them*

... Do not become idolaters as [they] did ... [They] sat down to eat and drink, and they rose up to play. The pressures and tensions of that challenging journey through unknown territory were tremendous. The Israelites had left a familiar past. No one knew what was ahead. Weariness brought anxiety, fear, anger. Such emotion tempted people to abandon all restraint, all self-discipline. Sometimes passion reigned supreme.

To point to signs of this condition in today's world elicits resentful accusations of moralizing and self-righteousness. But the facts speak for themselves. We see the loosening of many moral principles, the abandoning of boundaries on behaviour, the accepting of personal desire as the sole basis for choice and action. In what seems to be our contemporary wilderness, we are aware of living under the same pressures that oppressed those wandering Israelites of long ago.

Paul tells his listeners in Corinth that, as their empire and their culture change, they too are experiencing a time of endings and beginnings. He refers to *us, on whom the ends of the ages have come.* We know only too well that we live in a similar time of great and testing transition, in every aspect of life. For us also, much is ending and much is beginning. We all need to be vigilant as to how we respond to the many consequent pressures, both in personal and professional life. As Paul puts it, we need to hear the advice: *If you think you are standing, watch out that you do not fall.*

Here Paul is at his wisest and most pastoral. He communicates a sensitivity toward human nature and the many challenges we must wrestle with. *No testing has overtaken you that is not common to everyone. God is faithful, and he will not let you be tested beyond your strength, but with the testing he will also provide the way out so that you may be able to endure it.* This is a wonderfully enabling and encouraging insight. The most common illusion about much of our distress is that we are alone in the struggle. To realize that many others share this struggle relieves us of the need to feel uniquely guilty or culpable. Paul speaks to this reassuringly. He also reminds us of perhaps the most important thing of all — that grace is available to us as we continue our struggle, either as individuals or as a people of God.

The Gospel

We hear a conversation between Jesus and some people around him. We can assume that some or all of the disciples are present. The important thing is that we are here, too.

There were some present who told him about the Galileans whose blood Pilate mingled with their sacrifices. Someone mentions the latest incident of violence, knowing that Jesus will be concerned to hear about it, because people from his part of the country were involved. There has been another of the constant clashes with Pilate's military police. It is like those incidents we constantly hear about in Jerusalem today. Jesus decides to use the moment for teaching. *Do you think that because these Galileans suffered … they were worse sinners than all other Galileans?* He then links this reference with another one. Recently a building collapsed in the area and killed some workers. Jesus includes them in his question. *[Do you think] those eighteen who were killed when the tower … fell on them … were worse offenders than all … others?*

Our Lord is dealing with an ancient — maybe a timeless — human temptation to link disaster or suffering with culpability. Such and such has happened to someone. There must be a reason. It must be retribution for something he or she has done. Within hours of writing this reflection, I met someone who is a magnificent Christian. In recent years, she has had to bear an extraordinary amount of suffering. We had not met for some time. "You know that I now have to wrestle with a tumour?" she asked. Then she added laughingly, "I must have been very bad in a former incarnation." Her tone was light and courageous, but there was still that instinctual assumption of culpability, however joking.

To this our Lord brings a definite and resounding, *No, I tell you.* However, he immediately moves to another emphasis. *Unless you repent, you will all perish just as they did.* I am going to risk a suggestion here. The words sound harsh, but suppose they were said with a smile. If this were so, then I think our Lord is expressing a truth about life that we all know. To repent means to turn, to turn away from one thing to another, to change direction. There can be many times and many circumstances in our lives when, if we do not change direction, we will indeed "perish." If we persist in a certain course of action, we will lose a job, a reputation, a relationship. So what does our Lord mean here? Perhaps we should look at the story he tells as illustration.

A man had a fig tree … and he came looking for fruit on it and found none. Presumably each of us, like the fruit tree, is given life for a purpose — to bear fruit of some kind. What might this mean? What fruit is our Lord referring to? In specific terms, the meaning will differ according to our gifts, our choices, and the circumstances of our lives. But in general, our Lord must be asking that, as the tree gives its fruit for those around it, so our lives will be lived in giving to others, rather than in living for ourselves alone. To live in utter self-centredness is to die. To turn from such a barren life — to change — is to repent.

The different responses of the gardener and the owner of the vineyard are intriguing. Obviously the owner judges more swiftly than the gardener! *Cut it down! Why should it be wasting the soil?* Still, even the owner has waited for three years.

Our Lord seems to be saying that God is prepared to wait for our emergence from self-centredness. When we do so, turning from self to others, we thereby begin our turning to God. To do this, we are given many opportunities, much guidance and encouragement. However, there comes a time when a choice has been made. We are formed into who we are. It is too late to change direction, to repent. Something in us dies. But a loving and caring God has not brought about this inner dying. We have chosen it, and brought it about, ourselves. In this sense, we ourselves are the gardener. We are responsible to tend the soul that God has given.

Fourth Sunday in Lent

Joshua 5:9–12
Psalm 32
2 Corinthians 5:16–21
Luke 15:1-3, 11b–32

Weavings

These readings sing with themes of reconciliation, moments of joyful transition, and of homecoming.

First Reading. The people of Israel cross an invisible line separating Egypt and Israel. They have arrived in their land.

The Psalm. For the psalmist, acknowledging a sin has made all the difference.

Second Reading. For Paul, to have encountered Jesus Christ is to have become a new person.

The Gospel. The younger son, exiled by his own will, realizes who he is, and exile ends.

Reflections

First Reading

The Lord said to Joshua, "Today I have rolled away from you the disgrace of Egypt." Moses, Miriam, Pharaoh, the Nile, the days of forced labour, are all now stories to be passed on to children. The journey has been long and costly.

They kept the passover ... in the plains of Jericho. The moment we hear the word "Jericho," we know that this journey is far from over. Only the first stage, the wilderness stage, has ended. Sinai is far to the south. They are now looking west toward Jericho in the distance. The very sight is attractive and exciting. After long years in the desert, Jericho looks like Paradise. But possessing the city is still in the future. Important now is the fact that they are completely free of Egypt. They are beyond its farthest borders. The "disgrace" of it has been left behind.

To symbolize this crossing over to freedom from the last vestiges of bondage, they celebrate their first Passover in the new land. This is the first of two meals: one symbolic and resonant with history, the other actual and full of joy and satisfaction. For the very first time *they ate the produce of the land.* The writer's expression suggests how fervent this celebration was. He tells us precisely what they ate — *unleavened cakes and parched grain* — as if savouring every morsel.

He leaves us in no doubt whatsoever as to how they feel about leaving the manna of the desert! Once is not enough to say, *The manna ceased.* He has to say it twice more in different ways. *The Israelites no longer had manna; they ate the crops of the land of Canaan that year.* One can almost hear the songs and see the dancing as the campfires blaze.

The Psalm

About a year ago I picked up the phone and a familiar voice cried out, "I've just heard the news. He's not guilty!" For some months the case had gone on, dragging through the judicial system. It hung over a whole family, not just the accused. Now I heard immense relief and joy. Two words had changed everything: "Not guilty."

There are many kinds of guilt. There is the guilt we heap on ourselves for some word or action. We would give anything to unsay or undo whatever it was. That kind of guilt can eat away at us. *Happy are they whose transgressions are forgiven and whose sin is put away!* Here is the theme of this psalm. Someone has emerged from bearing a heavy load of guilt. Now this person revels in a new-found freedom from guilt. *Happy are they to whom the Lord imputes no guilt.*

For a long time, the guilt was carried inside, but at great cost. *While I held my tongue, my body wasted away through my groaning all the day long ... my bones withered away ... my moisture was dried up as by the heat of summer.* Many of us know these symptoms — a kind of aching inside oneself, a sense of things bearing down, a deep listlessness and lack of interest in life — the dark companions of unexpressed guilt.

Now comes the moment when the burden cannot be borne any longer, and must be shared. We are not told what brings on this decision. Suddenly it is there. *I said, "I will confess my transgressions to the Lord."* Notice how there is instantly a sense of being forgiven. The very next words tell us that the Lord *forgave me the guilt of my sin.*

The psalmist immediately wants to share his release with others. *Be glad, you righteous, and rejoice in the Lord; shout for joy, all who are true of heart.* As we listen, we realize that we have again heard a testimony to the healing power of confession — renewing, re-energizing, giving back life.

Second Reading

I remember once reading that, in the Middle Ages on a certain feast day, someone paraded through the streets while someone else went before calling out repeatedly, "Make way for the image of God!" I mention this because of the first sentence of this passage, a sentence typical of the subtlety of Paul's mind. *We regard no one from a human point of view; even though we once knew Christ from a human point of view, we know him no longer in that way.* Paul is saying that, precisely because we witnessed the human in Christ, we are now enabled to witness the divine in others. Why? Because those who have chosen to be of Christ carry his image within them.

But the consequences of choosing Christ as Lord go beyond this. *If anyone is in Christ, there is a new creation.* Notice Paul is not saying that, if anyone is in Christ, he or she is a new creation! He says, *There is a new creation.* In other words, choosing Christ as Lord affects how we see the world. We perceive reality in a new way, perhaps for the first time as it really is. We see "a new creation."

Paul continues, *God ... reconciled us to himself through Christ.* In other words, our human nature (which is unreconciled to God when we serve our own will) was lived by our Lord in such a way that it became an instrument for God's will rather than a rival, or even an enemy, of God's will. There is a lovely phrase in a prayer sometimes used at the end of the eucharistic rite. "When we were still far off, you met us in your Son and brought us home." This is what Paul is saying to us.

But then he adds something very important. *God ... has given us the ministry of reconciliation.* We have received a gift, and now we must share it. What does it mean to share a ministry of reconciliation? Paul tells us that our *trespasses are not counted against us.* There is no pretending that trespasses do not exist. They will always exist in our all too human lives. But God simply does not count them against us!

For this gift, God asks a response — that we live the same attitude toward others. God *[entrusts] the message of reconciliation to us.* Paul is writing this to the Corinthian community, but as scripture it is directed toward us.

Paul tells us something immensely significant about ourselves. If we have indeed chosen Jesus as our Lord, then each of us has become *the righteousness of God.* This means that, even though disagreement and antagonism may stress our relationships to the breaking point, yet we must understand one another as embodying *the righteousness of God.* Immediately we say this, we realize how this understanding is a dire necessity in today's church, so torn and weakened by disagreements and antagonisms!

The Gospel

Great moments like this challenge both someone who is preaching and someone who is studying or meditating. So much has been said, and so much written. How can one walk this path again, with the father and the two sons, and retrieve new insight?

There was a man who had two sons. Is it possible that in every one of us there are two offspring, and that this could be one reason for the timeless power of this parable? Let's pursue this thought and see where it leads. *The younger ... said ... "Give me the share ... that will belong to me."* There something in us impatient of waiting, wanting to possess now, to see now, to explore now, to grasp life now.

The younger son ... travelled to a distant country. There is something in us dissatisfied with what is, frustrated with here and now, with the familiar folk around us, the indescribable dullness of our surroundings. We long for another country. It doesn't really matter where, as long as it is elsewhere.

He squandered his property in dissolute living. There is the heady feeling of freedom, of being able to express who we really are. The truth is, of course, that this is far from freedom. It is merely an expression of appetite, an exhilarating discovery of what we conceive to be our rights. We are not really finding our self. We are merely discovering the self-centredness that lies within the self and waits for expression.

A severe famine took place ... and he began to be in need. The dryness and the emptiness spread across the landscape of the soul. Then comes a day when, as *he came to himself,* we also find our self. This happens after we have slowly and painfully worked out one of the great equations of life. We have discovered, at last, that rights without responsibilities are a *cul de sac.* When this realization comes, we want to go home — not to a distant place, but to our own true and whole self. What then becomes important is whether we have it in ourselves to forgive ourselves, whether the "older" one in us can forgive the wandering child in us, and welcome us home, as does the father in our Lord's story. *He ran and put his arms around him and kissed him.*

Sometimes it is not easy to come home to one's self. Another part of us begins to appear, the elder child within, the responsible part of us, the part that feels guilty for what has taken place, that is shamed by the discovery of the wandering younger one within. The *elder son was in the field ... he heard music and dancing ... He became angry and refused to go in.* Righteousness precludes forgiveness. A whole host of things — all good and admirable in themselves — emerge in the guise of their own shadows. Loyalty emerges as jealousy, consistency as rigidity, responsibility as self-righteousness. Such shadows refuse to sit down at the table of celebration; they refuse to join the dance. Negative elements within us can sometimes prevent us from coming home. At least they can prevent us from experiencing our homecoming as joy and forgiveness.

I am tempted to look at the story in this way, because I have always felt that, since the story is complete without the episode of the older brother, there must be some very good reason for our Lord to have introduced him. We try very hard to read the end of the chapter in a way that lets the party go on, but as we listen to the pleading of the father, we realize that the party cannot continue in quite the same way. *Son ... all that is mine is yours. But we had to celebrate ... this brother of yours was dead and has come to life.* Love is always mingled with some pain. Coming to oneself may be necessary and good, but the self we come to is never totally satisfying. I sometimes think that the father in the story is the self beyond my own self, the self of a loving God in Christ who can declare forgiveness even when the warring elements of my own self cannot.

Fifth Sunday in Lent

Isaiah 43:16–21
Psalm 126
Philippians 3:4b–14
John 12:1–8

Weavings

In every reading something of great worth has been or is about to be achieved or won, but in every case the victory is one with great cost.

First Reading. The crossing of the Red Sea has meant safety and hope to a people. But to another people, the cost has been defeat and loss.

The Psalm. A great breakthrough has been achieved. There is joy and celebration, but not without the price of some tears.

Second Reading. For Paul, the pearl of great price is to possess Jesus Christ, yet gaining that possession has meant the necessary loss of other things.

The Gospel. Just as the loving gesture of Mary is shadowed by the sour remark of Judas, so our Lord's vision of the kingdom of God is clouded by the coming price of suffering and death.

Reflections

First Reading

Even from this short passage, it is obvious that Isaiah would have been a consummate script writer for our media world so based on images! Not a syllable is wasted; every word flashes a scene before our eyes. We are watching the sea crossing that will shape the life and thought of the Israelites forever. For them it will always be *the Lord, who makes a way in the sea, a path in the mighty waters.*

Interestingly our camera lens is not trained on the people of Israel as they negotiate the soft oozing flood plain. Instead, we stand among the Egyptian pursuers, hearing the shouts of men as they desperately try to bring flailing horses under control, to free chariot wheels from the mud, knowing the deadly danger of these tidal waters. In a sentence, Isaiah conveys the extent of the disaster for them. We can almost hear the silence following the tumult, the calm of the returning tide as it covers the mortal agony of the enemy: *They lie down, they cannot rise, they are extinguished, quenched like a wick.*

Then, from the awful silence, we hear the first sound of triumph for those who have escaped. For them life has begun again. *Do not remember the former things.* For them, like a bad dream, captivity is over. Ahead is the wilderness (itself to be at times another bad dream, but in a different way). There is a sense of breakthrough. *I am about to do a new thing.* Their inner voice sounds confident about the future. They can deal with the looming wilderness because God *will make a way in the wilderness and rivers in the desert.* Already they are sublimely aware of a new identity. They may be poor, ill nourished, weakened by years of forced labour, but this no longer is the primary truth about them. From now on they are a people of whom God says, *I formed [them] for myself.* They even have a new vocation — by their very existence *to declare [God's] praise.*

At fearful cost, a victory has been won. It is probably true that all worthwhile victories in life are won at great cost. As we worship in these coming days, moving toward and then through the events of our Lord's passion, death, and resurrection, we will witness the terrible cost of the greatest of all victories, the victory over death.

The Psalm

Nothing in life is quite so wonderful as something longed for and then received contrary to all expectation — the surprising gift, the unexpected breakthrough, the recovery long despaired of.

Contrary to all expectation, something has happened to *[restore] the fortunes of Zion.* The whole society is ecstatic: *Our mouth [was] filled with laughter.* Given the realities of time and place, the cause may have been success in battle. There is a hint that victory has not come without cost. We are given a glimpse of *those who sowed with tears ... those who go out weeping.* But the event could also have been a program of reform or the signing of a treaty promising security. The point is its unexpectedness — the people are *like those who dream.* Obviously, the surrounding societies are just as surprised, because they too are saying in wonderment that *the Lord has done great things for them.*

The psalmist now uses a vivid image that tells us a great deal about the situation. He likens this event to *the watercourses of the Negev.* The point is that, at certain seasons, these watercourses are bone dry. There is not the slightest hint that they will ever flow again; they may not flow for years. Then suddenly, there will come a rushing cascade that sweeps all before it. The image is one of unexpectedness. We will know this kind of experience when we witness our Lord on the cross in the days fast approaching in our worship. Resurrection is shattering because of its total unexpectedness.

In this psalm, someone is singing to us about the difference that can be made in life by our capacity to hope. We are a society where much looks barren, where tears are more common than laughter. For many today, cynicism is felt to be an indication of sophistication. But believing men and women are committed to the possibility that the future is always open to unexpected inroads and influences that can sweep us in constructive directions. In the language of the psalmist, we are called to be a people who believe that the Lord can do great things for us because *the Lord has done great things for us.*

Second Reading

In the middle of what is probably the happiest of his letters, Paul writes a very painful reflection on his own life. He realizes that some people in the Philippi community fervently wish the old way of physical circumcision to continue. Paul is anxious to show how this *confidence in the flesh* is rooting the source of grace primarily in oneself. He now decides to be very honest about his own claim to such confidence, a claim he has set aside for reasons he will write in a few moments. For now, in a very precise way, as if each phrase is being wrung unwillingly from him, he spells out why he could make such a claim himself. *Circumcised on the eighth day, a member of the people of Israel, of the tribe of Benjamin, a Hebrew born of Hebrews; as to the law, a Pharisee; as to zeal* (we can almost feel his pain as he prepares to write these next words) *a persecutor of the church* (then adding bitterly, because of the irony of it all) *as to righteousness under the law, blameless.*

Now comes his gain and his loss — one cannot come without the other. To gain Christ he had had to deliberately let go of the tradition in which he was formed. *For his sake I have suffered the loss of all things.* For Paul, this immense act of renunciation of everything that had meaning for him is paramount. *I regard them as rubbish, in order that I may gain Christ.* And what is the great gift he has gained? *A righteousness ... [not] of my own, but one that comes through faith in Christ.* He is so anxious that his readers understand what he is saying that he repeats his statement in other words: *the righteousness from God based on faith.*

I suspect that this is one of the moments when the floodgates of emotion open in Paul. I think, if we could hear him, he would be speaking to us with great intensity. This is the heart of things as he understands them. *I want to know Christ and the power of his resurrection and the sharing of his sufferings by becoming like him in his death.* One cannot help noticing how every phrase is oriented away from Paul himself toward our Lord. Four times he points beyond himself in the words "Christ ... his ... his ... him."

Now we hear the wonderful realism of Paul, a realism that gives hope to every soul trying to walk the Christian way. Notice that he says, *If somehow I may attain the resurrection from the dead. Not that I have already obtained this ... but I press on.* What encouragement for us who sometimes feel so far away from any such state as obtaining our Lord's resurrection power! But there is even more encouragement for a Christian here. Paul says that, even though he has by no means arrived at any great spiritual achievement, he receives grace to keep pressing on *because Christ Jesus has made me his own.* It is as if Paul is explaining a crazy wonderful, almost unbelievable, paradoxical truth — that we may never come close to the mountain top that is Christ, yet we have already arrived because he has made us *his own.* Thanks be to God!

The Gospel

There they gave a dinner for him. There is something fascinating about this simple statement. Our own experience reminds us what such occasions entail. From what we already know of Martha, we can see her bustling about, giving orders, expressing exasperation with this and that, anxious about having everything just as it should be for guests. We know she is a naturally hospitable person. The first time Jesus passed their house, it was she who had invited him in. Martha had complained then about Mary's ability to stay away from household chores. One cannot help wondering if that episode of some months ago had had any effect on Mary's participation! The phrase, *Martha served,* would seem to indicated that it had not!

How fascinating it would be to have been given the guest list for this night. Only one guest is named, the mysterious figure of Lazarus, about whom no word is said and from whom no word comes.

Now the moment arrives for which this meal will always be remembered. At some point in the evening Mary rises, approaches the guest of honour, kneels before him, and anoints his feet. This is no casual gesture. John tells us that *Mary took a pound of costly perfume made of pure nard.* When we realize that nard was imported from as far away as the Himalayas, we can begin to imagine what it had cost her.

The silence is brutally shattered by Judas' tasteless itemizing of the exact cost of the gift that had been given, at the same time dismissing contemptuously the use to which the gift had been put. *Why was this perfume not sold for three hundred denarii and the money given to the poor?* Years later, as he writes this part of his gospel, John's anger boils over when he recalls this moment. He cannot resist remarking that Judas *said this, not because he cared for the poor, but because he was a thief.*

Our Lord's response is immediate and sharp. We can hear this in the words, *Leave her alone.* Then perhaps his voice becomes lower, softer, gentler. Perhaps there is a note of sadness, even fear, as he says, *She bought it so that she might keep it for the day of my burial.* We can be almost certain that there was a stunned silence. In this silence, Jesus looks directly at Judas as he says, not without a touch of bitterness, *You always have the poor with you, but you do not always have me.*

As we move toward the events to come in the next couple of weeks, we are given this most human moment. Our Lord is doing what all of us love to do — sit at a table with friends. This house at Bethany was for Jesus the treasured place of friendship. Such moments must have been for him piercing reminders of the cost of the decision he was making. His humanity must have rebelled against the possibility of death, just as ours does. The gesture of Mary, probably coming from a deep affection if not a passionate love, must also have reminded him of what he was sacrificing by taking the road that led to danger and confrontation and death. The fact that he must already have had some suspicions about Judas' intentions added to the deep hurt of this evening.

All of these things pointed to the awful cost of his faithfulness to his own vision of the kingdom of God. Victory there would eventually be, but a most costly victory. If we seek reasons to offer him our gratitude, let it be for his willingness to pay this great cost.

Liturgy of the Passion

Isaiah 50:4–9a
Psalm 31:9–16
Philippians 2:5–11
Luke 22:14–23:56

Weavings

In every reading we are in the presence of someone who knows that a dreadful ordeal must be faced and who seeks and finds the grace to face it.

First Reading. The fact that the servant of God has to set his face like a flint is the measure of his fear in the face of the challenge ahead.

The Psalm. The poet does not even try to disguise his distress. He is beyond being able to do so. His only recourse is utter trust in God.

Second Reading. Here a terrible sacrifice is made. The majestic serenity of the one who makes it points to his greatness.

The Gospel. The hour for our Lord's sacrifice has come. We follow the sequence of events, and see that he never falters in his decision and purpose.

Reflections

First Reading

We cannot identify the person to whom we are listening. It may be the prophet himself or someone to whom he is referring. What we do know is that this person has a deep sense of being God's servant in the situation where he finds himself. Even this is spiritual instruction for us. The whole point of our lives as Christians is to possess and live out such an attitude.

We can assume a certain context for this passage. The people of God are still in exile in Babylon. As God's servant, this person has tried to reach them with what he deems to be a message from God. It would seem that this message is received with resentment and even violent rejection. *I gave my back to those who struck me, and my cheeks to those who pulled out the beard; I did not hide my face from insult and spitting.* Presumably these insults are the more painful because they are inflicted by his own people.

We realize the quality of this person's resolve when we see how unrelentingly the pressure of his task bears upon him. *Morning by morning [God] wakens my ear to listen.* What he hears each morning sends him back to the extremely difficult mission he has been given, one that his people are simply not prepared to accept.

So what makes it possible for him to return again and again to the struggle? No less than four times he tells us. *The Lord has given me the tongue of a teacher [verse 4]. The Lord God has opened my ear [verse 5]. The Lord God helps me [verse 7]. It is the Lord God who helps me [verse 9].* The very reiteration of God's assurances seems to make him stronger. *I have not been disgraced ... I have set my face like flint ... Who are my adversaries? Let them confront me.*

We are seeing in this passage a model for what we are about to see in our Lord. Centuries will go by before our Lord comes to his passion and death, but when he does, we recognize in Jesus the pattern framed by this long-ago suffering servant of God. Even more, from various statements of our Lord, we know that he himself looked back to Isaiah and the portraits of this suffering servant, seeing them as patterns that he wished to emulate and act out in his own ministry.

The Psalm

It is possible to see the first reading and the psalm as showing us opposite sides, or moods, of a time of struggle in our lives. All of us know the way our inward struggling goes. For a while we are determined to prevail. There is a mood of confidence and optimism. Then a different mood sweeps over us. We feel overcome by what we have to deal with. This mood in turn gives way again to confidence or hope.

If the first reading shows us someone who rallies in the face of his struggle, the psalm confronts us immediately with an atmosphere of absolute hopelessness. *I am in trouble, my eye is consumed with sorrow ... my life is wasted with grief ... my strength fails ... my bones are consumed.* The sense of desperation continues unrelentingly. *I have become a reproach to all my enemies ... and ... neighbours, a dismay to those of my acquaintance.*

The mood changes to one of craven fear. *I hear the whispering of the crowd ... [as] they put their heads together against me.* At this point, the psalmist reaches out for help. *I [trust] in you, O Lord.* The entreaties continue. The short phrases suggest that he is gasping out his pleas as one struggling for breath. *You are my God! ... My times are in your hand! ... rescue me ... Make your face to shine upon your servant! ... and in your loving-kindness save me.* But in these verses, there is no sign of response to his pleas. We see only a desperate human being imploring help.

Because we are in Passiontide, our thoughts naturally go to our Lord when we read this psalm. In its verses, we can almost hear his thoughts as he endures the terrible hours on the cross, those hours that brought him to his great cry of anguish: *My God! My God! Why have you forsaken me?*

Second Reading

Let the same mind be in you that was in Christ Jesus. When we first hear Paul's counsel, there is a certain reasonableness about it. After all, if we claim to be Christian, we should strive to be like our Lord. Only when we look again, seeing exactly what Paul means, do we realize the terrifying standard we are being set!

What was the mind of Christ as described in the following lines? Let us spell out one by one the decisions he made. He *emptied himself.* He took *the form of a slave.* He was *born in human likeness. He humbled himself and became obedient to the point of death.* The degree of self-sacrifice is so colossal that it leaves us in awe. Are we ever remotely able to act with this kind of self-sacrifice? We know the answer only too well.

But it is precisely the depth of sacrifice in his obedience that leads to the height of glory our Lord attained. These lines are like the crashing of a great chorus that gets louder and louder. *The name that is above every name ... every knee should bend ... every tongue confess.*

What is most important to see here is that, in the domain of God, power emerges from humility. Ultimate authority is won by ultimate obedience.

The Gospel

When one is faced with a gospel passage of this length, we are also faced with certain consequences for homilizing, studying, or meditating. First is the time factor, arising from the length of the passage. Second is the sheer variety of locations and events in the passage.

My suggestion is that we look at the reading as a film with succeeding sets and scenes. This will help us to do it reasonable justice in the time we may have. I also suggest that, since the reading is part of the core narrative of our faith (I say "part of" only for the obvious reason that it does not contain the resurrection event), it would be a good idea to treat it as essentially narrative.

Here are two possible ways if we wish to contain the whole sequence of the narrative.

First way: List the actual locations to which we are taken by the sequence. There are at least seven locations (eight, if the council meeting was not held in the house of the High Priest).

Second way: In each of these locations we meet a particular person. Let us virtually meet these people, and see if they embody aspects of ourselves and our human nature.

Let us look at the first possible way of considering the narrative. The places or locations are the Upper Room, the garden in Gethsemane, the house of the High Priest, the Judgement Hall of Pilate (twice), the town residence of Herod, the streets leading to crucifixion (the Via Dolorosa), the place of execution (the Skull).

I would suggest that we now look at these places, trying to define them in terms of what our Lord experienced in each of them. For instance, the Upper Room is the place of community; Gethsemane, the place of vulnerability; the High Priest's house, the place of confrontation. Pilate's hall I would suggest we call the place of the powers; Herod's town house, the place

of decadence; the Via Dolorosa, the place of suffering and loneliness. The hill is the place of dying.

We now could begin to reflect on what our Lord experienced in these places — desperately needing community, feeling totally vulnerable, confronting enemies, facing the power
structures of his society, and so on. Then we may wish to apply
such experiences to our own human experience, asking what
these things may mean for us in our time.

The second way I have mentioned is to look at each of the
particular people who emerge in each of the locations. In the
upper room it is Peter. In Gethsemane it may be Judas. In the
High Priest's house it is Ciaphas himself; in the judgement hall,
Pilate; in the town house, Herod. On the way through the streets,
it is Simon from Cyrene; on the hill, either thief or both thieves.
We might look at these people one by one, quickly and simply
considering the part they take in this drama — the human weaknesses they show, the moral dilemmas some of them face. Taken
together, they demonstrate a wide spectrum of our human nature.

What might be the real feelings of Peter, when he protests
his loyalty to Jesus in the upper room? What might it signify
that, of all the ways of identifying Jesus, Judas chooses a kiss?
What are the pressures on Pilate? Why does he react as he does?
The same question goes for Ciaphas. Neither of these men is a
simple dyed-in-the-wool villain. They are experienced and responsible public figures. What happens to them inside themselves?

This method of approach deals only with some possibilities. For instance, one could say that, in the scene in the house
of the High Priest, it is not so much Peter who emerges for our
attention as it is the servant girl. In what way can we interpret
her momentary entry onto the stage of the drama? I mention
this only to point out another possibility.

In this second way, as in the first, the point is to see if these
incidents are at all woven into the fabric of our own experience.

Easter Day

Isaiah 65:17–25
Psalm 118:1–2, 14–24
Acts 10:34–43 or 1 Corinthians 15:19–26
John 20:1–18

Whether we are homilizing from the pulpit, studying with others, or meditating in one's own home, working with the readings for this day presents considerable challenge. For many people, this is one of the few occasions when they will attend public worship. How does a preacher fully express the resurrection faith without betraying the mystery of the cross, and all in the context of a liturgy that is already long? For most Christians, the resurrection is an enduringly problematical issue. How does an individual or group wrestle with the meaning and implication of the risen Christ in the context of everyday life?

I am finding, in recent years, that when we are faced with the great central mysteries of the faith — Easter, Christmas, Pentecost, Transfiguration, Good Friday (and you may wish to add others), the best method of approach is by far the oldest of all ways — story. When we resort to story, we begin to understand or communicate at a level beyond the merely rational and intellectual. We could spend a long time reflecting about the significance and power of story. The best way to judge for yourself is to try it.

As an experiment, let me move away from the format I have followed for other Sundays. My suggestion is that we might best present the scriptures in reverse order — gospel, second lesson (choosing Acts), and then the Isaiah passage. Here is one way to attempt this.

Reflections

I would like us to meet a woman, a young woman, probably somewhere in her late twenties or early thirties. She has had a kind of "up and down" life. There have been tough times. She has known emotional storms and failed relationships. But about two years ago, something peculiar happened. She met an unusual person.

Life changed when she met this man. There was no sudden passionate love affair, although she probably loved him deeply. But when she was with him, she felt herself somehow to be healed. After a while, whether she was with him or not, she knew that she had indeed been healed.

If you had asked her what he gave her, she probably would have had to search for an answer. In her groping response, she might have used the word "kingdom," or maybe the word "vision" or "dream." We don't know for sure. But she would look far-away and say quietly, "He gave me a vision of a new world, where I was different and people were different and relationships were different, even, in a strange way, all of nature was different." And when someone would ask, "Different in what way?" she would grope again for words and say, "He seemed to be asking me to imagine what the world would be like if God's will was always and everywhere obeyed. He called it the kingdom of God."

Time went by for this young woman. She gave a great deal of her time to be with the man. By now there was a community of men and women who had begun to share the same vision. So

Mary — that was her name— left the village of Magdala by the lake and followed him and them. And for about two years, things went reasonably smoothly.

Only reasonably. There were unpleasant times — arguments, disagreements, sometimes an insulting crowd, sometimes even some danger. He moved through it all, although not without stress and cost.

But then everything changed. Gradually there were more enemies than friends. The danger became immediate and frightening. Afterwards she would remember those weeks and days as if they had been a dream, a very different dream, a terrible dream.

There came the day she would carry for the rest of her life. She was on a slope across from a small hill. On the hill were three of the obscene crosses the Romans used everywhere, and on one of them the man she loved was writhing and moaning like a wounded animal. His body was naked, his face drawn and white. He had lost all control because of the unbelievable pain. She stayed there until evening, until she saw his body taken down by friends, and she watched where he was laid to rest. She left the place, went to her lodging, and tried to get some sleep.

It is at this point that we joined her this morning here in church. It is the first day of the week. It is not yet dawn. She has just reached the rock wall where she saw him placed. To her astonishment the rock has an opening. The stone is rolled back. She backs away terrified, then she runs.

She runs to where there are others who know her. She bursts in and hears herself shouting, "They've taken him. They've taken him." One of them holds her until they can make out what she means. As soon as they understand, they rush from the house, she with them.

John is younger. He gets there first but he hesitates; Peter rushes past him, lowers his head, and disappears into the darkness. John goes after him. They stand in the shadows, thunder-struck. They will remember this moment the rest of their lives. What they see is the linen that had wrapped the body. It lies on the stone slab, the head linen folded a little distance from it. There is no body. Speechless, they come out. They walk as if in shock. They seem unaware that Mary is there.

She waits in the silence, her sobbing the only sound. She stoops to look in. For her, instead of shadows, there is a blazing light. It seems focused where she has been expecting to tend his body. It is as if the light itself is questioning the necessity for her weeping. She steps back into the open air, hears a voice, and turns. The figure in the shadows could be anyone. Again she hears the same voice questioning her weeping. This time she pleads for pity. If his body is available, could she please be taken to it? Then she hears her name, and her world blazes with the same light that she has seen in the tomb.

That evening she makes her way back into the city. This time there is no running, no shouting, no sobbing. The news is too great, too joyful. She looks at them and they at her. She says quietly, *I have seen the Lord,* and her face and her voice are such that there are no questions.

All this happened a long time ago. She was never the same again, neither were Peter nor John, who ran with her that day. A few weeks later, the same Peter, who by this time had seen the risen Christ more than once, stood up in front of a crowd and told his story.

Someone else told the story of a wonderful transforming event in the images of a beautiful dream. The name of the person who had that dream was Isaiah. He lived a long time before Jesus of Nazareth, but both of them shared the dream of a kingdom. In their dream, they saw a kingdom of beauty, peace, and joy, a kingdom they would have called *shalom.* And they knew that this kingdom came from the rule and the will of God.

But, you see, we also dream this same dream. It will never die. Even though we can never make it fully come true, it calls people in every generation to work for its fulfillment. Every thought that has integrity, every action that reaches for justice. Everything we do to include rather than exclude, to create rather than destroy. Every act of love rather than hate, every creation of beauty rather than ugliness. All these things come from this dream and help to bring it into reality.

At the heart of the dream is the one who dreamed it, who died for it, and who in a way we will never understand, moved through death to call us to dream the dream, and to build that kingdom of God in our own lives and in our own society and time.

If you could have asked Mary of Magdala what she believed, she would have said simply, *He is risen.* Peter and John would also have answered, *He is risen.* If in each generation over the following twenty centuries you had asked, "What do people believe about all this," millions of people would have answered you, "Jesus Christ is risen."

Today, in a world that sometimes seems very different from any world before it, it is still possible to ask, "What do you believe?" and millions of men and women reply to you, "Jesus Christ is risen." What you yourself say in reply to that question has to be your choice. The irony, of course, is this, that whether or not you and I believe that it is so, it is still true that Jesus Christ is risen. Alleluia!

Second Sunday of Easter

Acts 5:127–32
Psalm 150
Revelation 1:4–8
John 20:19–31

Weavings

As the echoes of our Lord's resurrection still resound, we are conscious of the existence of a new reality — the church.

First Reading. The first instinct of the newborn community is to mission, even in the face of resistance.

The Psalm. Of the two psalms suggested, I have chosen psalm 150 because it expresses the understandable joy of this season.

Second Reading. Once again our awareness is directed to the new reality of the church, now already growing in the areas to which John writes.

The Gospel. The early community crouches behind locked doors, but the risen Lord is not limited by such barriers.

Reflections

First Reading

No sooner is the embryonic Christian community born than it encounters a strong dose of political reality. It confronts a kind of law in human affairs. Any new force acting in a society or an institution will meet resistance from forces already entrenched. *The High Priest took action; he and all who were with him ...* Already we are using the language of "with" and "against." Neither do we see the gentle disagreement characteristic of some church affairs. *They arrested the apostles and put them in the public prison.*

We can only guess at the source of rescue. *An angel of the Lord opened the prison doors.* It may indeed have been an angel. Or one wonders what courageous supporter of the new movement was prepared to risk life and limb to make the angelic visit possible.

Now follows a small comedy of errors. News comes to the authorities that there is more trouble. Assuming that other members of the new community have caused the incident, the authorities send for their erstwhile prisoners, and are told not only that the prisoners have escaped, but that that they are the very troublemakers causing this second disturbance.

There is great significance in the fact that *they brought them, but without violence, for they were afraid of being stoned by the people.* Already the new movement was gathering considerable support.

We gave you strict orders ... yet here you have filled Jerusalem with your teaching. The High Priest is being reasonable, and for good reason. It is extremely desirable that there be no public disturbance. It is the last thing the authorities want, most of all the Roman authorities. Alas, the High Priest finds that he is not dealing with reasonable people. These people are intoxi-cated by the wine of resurrection. They are labouring under the illusion that their as yet small movement will change the world. Neither they nor the Temple priests realize that this is exactly what will happen!

What does the passage say to us? Perhaps it asks us a ques-tion. To what extent can we challenge the society of our day in Jesus' name? When we do encounter Christians who are pre-pared conscientiously to object, how can we support them? Per-haps the most important question arises when we remember that the early church got into trouble through its success in healing people. How can healing become once again a rich part of Christian experience?

The Psalm

These verses are full of celebration and ecstasy. They call an individual to jump for joy, unshackle the mind, and let the heart sing. They urge a congregation to leap out of the pews and dance in the aisles. They inspire the choir to sing out in full voice, and the organist to engage the full organ. The psalm should prob-ably be sung enough times for everyone to drop from exhaus-tion!

Exaggeration? Of course. And yet, are we being totally irre-sponsible to paint the above scenario? Probably yes — if we are talking about mainline Christian congregations from a West-ern cultural background. But it is quite possible to hear this scenario literally played out in many parts of the world. Cer-tainly in many parts of Africa it would be possible.

This psalm is very important for the churches of the late twentieth-century West. It is doing nothing less than demand-ing that we consider at least a measure of pentecostal fervour in our worship. But to speak of measuring out pentecostal fervour is a kind of contradiction, a nod to our cultural limitations. We cannot "dole out" the Holy Spirit on ourselves or on a congregation. If we tried, the congregation would be deafened by the Spirit's laughter!

How far beyond the domain of mere religion this psalm takes us! Praise is indeed to be given in God's *holy temple,* but we are pushed even beyond its walls. God is to be praised in the whole domain of creation, *in the firmament of [God's] power.* This done, God is to be praised in the whole process of time and history, the context of God's *mighty acts* and God's *excellent greatness.*

At last, the psalmist gathers together every conceivable order of life — rather like a musical Noah inviting all life into a vast ark of sound — and evokes an almost unimaginable shout of praise: *Let everything that has breath praise the Lord.*

Second Reading

John to the seven churches that are in Asia. The simple spare statement comes as a pleasant surprise. We feel like saying, "What? Only last week we celebrated our Lord's resurrection, and already we are reading about there being seven churches a thousand miles from Jerusalem!" Even when we remind ourselves that this passage was written about thirty or forty years after that first Easter, we still feel a certain thrill that the spread of the faith has begun. After all, joy does not always have to be based on logic!

How magnificent is the language of John. Kipling once wrote of those "who splash at a ten league canvas with a brush of comet's hair." John certainly does. There is surely no small God to be found here. *Who is and who was and who is to come.* This takes care of all of time — past, present, and future. The *seven spirits who are before his throne.* This covers the gamut of spiritual gifts that we want or need. *Jesus Christ, the faithful witness, the first-born of the dead, and the ruler of kings on earth.*

There is not a moment's hesitation in making claims for our Lord that will sweep across an empire, eventually outlive it, and then form the womb of future cultures and societies.

Suddenly the lens changes. We are swept in from far vistas to the world of the individual and the personal. God may be Lord of time, the spirits may hover at the heavenly throne, and Jesus may be the ruler of kings. But this same God, and the Holy Spirit made flesh in Jesus, comes to us as friend, giver of grace, and Saviour, as one *who loves us and freed us from our sins.*

Two other things we are told about our Lord. *He has made us to be a kingdom, priests serving his God and Father.* That is my vocation as a Christian, to offer myself to God in all ways that I can. *He is coming and every eye shall see him.* This is the reality by whom my life is measured and to whom I am accountable. To say this is not to be threatened, but to feel that one's life — so short, so ambiguous, so vulnerable, and at times so pathetic — has infinite meaning in God.

The Gospel

The doors were shut ... for fear. This tells us volumes. No nobility here, no courageous stances. This is the other side of human nature. Survival has become primary. Perhaps at times, such a stance is necessary, even wise. In today's church, there are times for shutting the doors — if by this, we mean gathering as a community to take stock and to plan. But such assessment and consideration should always result in finding new ways to open the doors as widely as possible. If our shutting of doors is *for fear,* then we need to consider very clearly and honestly what we fear. It is wise to remember the wisdom in the lines of William Cowper's hymn: "Ye fearful saints, fresh courage take;/The clouds ye so much dread/Are big with mercy, and shall break/with blessings on your head."

Jesus came and stood among them and said, ... "Peace be with you." Then the disciples rejoiced when they saw the Lord. When we think of closing doors, it is important to remember that the risen Lord is unaware of such things! He comes whether our doors are locked or wide open.

Jesus stood among them. This may seem a small thing to notice, but it points us to something. He did not stand before and above them, with all that such a stance suggests. He does not point toward something he himself is not equally involved in or committed to. Whatever they do, wherever they go, he will be among them.

Perhaps this is why his first gesture is to show them *his hands and his side.* What greater evidence that he is indeed among them, fully involved in all the costs and burdens of human experience. There is no greater comfort or encouragement than to know that someone you trust and love is truly with you and committed to you.

John tells us that Jesus brought *peace,* and that *the disciples rejoiced when they saw the Lord.* After the atmosphere in the room had changed, Jesus *breathed on them,* and said, *I send you.* As the disciples must have done, we also need constantly to ask, "Where is our Lord in this situation we face?" Just by asking this question, we at least open ourselves to the presence of our Lord. And if the presence is experienced, our fear can be changed to gladness, a measure of peace can be found, and we can become potential servants, ready to be sent to carry out a task. At such a moment, when we decide that our Lord is a risen reality to whom, as Thomas, we can give our loyalty in spite of all our doubts, then our Lord breathes on us and we receive the grace to do the tasks he gives us.

Third Sunday of Easter

Acts 9:1–6 (7–20)
Psalm 30
Revelation 5:11–14
John 21:1–19

Weavings

In very different forms and through the eyes of very different people, we are given three visions of the risen Lord.

First Reading. Saul, driven relentlessly by his determination to root out the new faith, receives a blinding vision of the Christ he hates.

The Psalm. The psalmist sings of moments in life when we experience many lesser deaths, and of moments when we rise to life again.

Second Reading. John draws aside a curtain to reveal the awesome majesty of God.

The Gospel. With disarming simplicity, the risen Lord encounters the disciples at the lakeshore they know so well.

Reflections

First Reading

We are at one of the great crossroads in history. As we listen to the sound of approaching horses, we prepare to witness a moment of incalculable change in human affairs. All seems normal among the group of riders until a sudden disturbance occurs. It is over so quickly that we hardly know whether it was light or sound or tremor. The horses rear, squealing in terror. A man lies grovelling on the road, groping, crying out. As we watch, he is helped to his feet. He is so shaken that he cannot mount his horse again. Humbled, slumped over, encountered devastatingly by the Christ he has so hatefully pursued, Saul is *led ... by the hand* down the road to the nearby city walls.

The conversion of the person who is ever afterward to be known as Paul is sudden and dramatic. Few of us experience such moments. But the scripture is saying to us that every Christian needs to be open to the possibility of a moment of encounter, when Christian faith becomes focused and a conscious decision is made to follow our Lord. It may not be literally true for us that *a light from heaven flashed*, but these words can describe those many moments when men and women suddenly realize that their Christian faith means infinitely more to them than they could ever have expected.

The second thing we need to notice is the circumstance in which the encounter takes place. *He was going along and approaching Damascus.* The call comes in the course of Saul's working day! In a sense, it comes (as we might say) at the office. This fact conflicts with our contemporary ideas of God, and things of God, as occupying mainly the private realm of our lives.

Likewise, we can see echoes for our experience in the exchange between Saul and the risen Christ, as Saul lies on the road. Saul asks, *Who are you, Lord?* There is not one of us who does not need to take some quiet time to ask this question. We are asking, "What does my Christian faith really mean to me? What do I really believe? To what extent does this faith form my life and my character?"

Sometimes there is so much in a tiny word in scripture. Notice something wonderful about our Lord's reply, especially the word *but* that comes at a certain point. In reply to Saul, Jesus says, *I am Jesus, whom you are persecuting.* Notice the bluntness of this. It must have pierced Saul to the quick. Then comes what I cannot help but call a glorious "but"! Jesus says, *But get up, and enter the city, and you will be told what to do.* It is as if Jesus were saying, "Yes, you have persecuted me, but that is past now. What matters is what happens from here on." How powerful those few words could be for so many of us — to hear our Lord saying, "Yes, this and that is true of your past, but get up, and you will be told what you are to do." We can hear our Lord saying, in effect, that it does not matter what we have been. It is over, done with, forgiven! What matters is what we can now be in his service and with his grace.

The Psalm

There are times when we experience mortal fear, when all we ask is that we can survive the threat. We are not concerned about pride or dignity. We ask, pray, plead, bargain. Whether or not we are the kind of person who uses religious language, we are in fact appealing to God, because we know that we are in the realm where life and death meet.

Such things are the substance of this psalm. *O Lord my God, I cried to you ... I was going down to the grave.* This is the language of doctors' offices and hospital corridors, of solitary walks with one's own lonely and terrible fears. At such times, we come to realize how much we take life for granted, how sweet its ordinary pleasures — especially when we face the possibility of losing them — and how naively we trust in our own strength and abilities. *While I felt secure, I said, "I shall never be disturbed." You, Lord ... made me as strong as the mountains.*

Then you hid your face. There is a sudden and shocking change in our lives. A phone rings, a letter arrives, a trusted relationship is betrayed, a carefully measured voice gives us a diagnosis. Light changes to darkness, music falls silent. Our own voice cries with the psalmist, *I go down to the Pit ... have mercy ... Lord, be my helper.*

Now comes the voice of other times we have known. *You have turned my wailing into dancing ... clothed me with joy.* We know the surge of returning life after a great shadow has been lifted. We want to share the good news. We find ourselves laughing, babbling our relief, as does the psalmist. *My heart sings to you ...* Now that the terror is lifted, we forget the hours of fear and worry. The threat, the feeling of life betraying us, the thought of God being angry for some reason — all seems now to be *but the twinkling of an eye.* The pleading and the promises are now memories: *O Lord my God, I will give thanks for ever.* If we dared to be completely truthful, such memories may be a trifle embarrassing. But whatever direction our lives may take after such an experience, we have now looked in a clear glass, and we have seen deeply into our humanity. We have learned of our need for grace beyond ourselves.

Second Reading

For John, as he writes, there is no image of the glorified Jesus richer than that of *the Lamb*. It is as if John invites us to follow Jesus through the veil of death, then through the more mysterious veil of resurrection, and finally into the very presence of God, where we encounter this same Jesus, now glorified in a way that defeats all language to describe it.

John's great gift for language communicates a sense of infinite space and light, power and splendour. The scene is almost beyond description or comprehension. Yet John focuses our gaze on the utter simplicity and familiarity of a single image — a lamb. This is how he wishes us to think about our Lord. Why? Because nothing embodies the concepts of vulnerability and sacrifice better than this animal. These are the concepts through which John reveals to us the great and terrible cost of the glory we now see. For John, Jesus is the one who sacrificed self utterly, who took on our human nature, who bowed himself to every aspect of humanity, even death itself. This is the reason for the great song, *"Worthy is the Lamb who was slain!"*

The song and the shout are expressions of a great mystery about the deep places of our human experience. It is a truth we have seen in lives around us and, perhaps, in our own life. To sacrifice the self for others is mysteriously the door to a glory we do not understand but we know to be true.

The Gospel

One of life's most memorable moments is to stand early in the morning on the north shore of the Lake of Galilee, knowing that you are somewhere near where this encounter took place.

I am going fishing. The words are replete with many feelings. There is a desire to do anything to escape from the terrible immobility that loss brings. There is the instinct to do what one knows best, what most fulfills one's gifts and strengths. There is the longing to exert some control over one's shattered life. All of this is reflected in Peter's simple statement and echoed in the voices that reply to him. John places the reply immediately after Peter's words. We can sense the alacrity, the eagerness, the relief of the others. *They said to him, "We will go with you."*

And so they do. All night they work, but nothing is gained until the dawn comes and a voice from the shore suggests a different direction, and there are fish everywhere! It is the intuitive John who first realizes what is happening. *It is the Lord!* Peter's response, true to character, is to say nothing but to act. He grabs his work clothes and jumps into the water, probably to wade ashore.

Bring some of the fish that you have just caught, says Jesus. Such simplicity is in every moment of this encounter. We hear our Lord speaking to our own experience. We can imagine our Lord saying to us again and again, "Bring me what you do, what you make, what you achieve. Bring me the best of yourself, and let me see what I can do with it." And if we do bring to our Lord who and what we are, we find that he can do things with it beyond our expectations.

Come and have breakfast. As a simple personal discipline, we might consider recalling these words when we go forward to receive Holy Communion. We do this most often in the morning. It can be a rich experience for us to remember that other morning — the lakeshore, the fire, the hand offering a piece of bread, a piece of fish. To kneel or stand before the altar, bowing one's head to the mystery of our Lord's presence, never nagging at the mystery, never trying to explain or analyze it, but always bowing one's head and saying to oneself, *It [is] the Lord* — such is the stuff of which close encounters with our Lord are made.

When they had finished breakfast. There now takes place one of the most intimate encounters of the whole gospel. I suggest that, to appreciate its full meaning and impact, we should link it to another passage. Let us recall the moment in the upper room when Jesus warns the disciples that Satan is going to *sift all of you like wheat.* He directs this warning to Peter, who stoutly denies that he will succumb. He assures Jesus that he is ready to go with him *to prison and to death.* Sadly, Jesus counters Peter's reply by saying that he will deny even knowing Jesus (Luke 22:31–34).

For weeks now, Peter has been living with the shame of what subsequently happened. Now he and his risen Lord meet again. Jesus calls Peter aside and they have the conversation we read today. Each time Jesus asks Peter the question, *Do you love me?* Jesus directs him to feed and tend his sheep.

Who are the sheep? I would suggest that Jesus is referring to the disciples clustered around the fire a little way down the beach. Could it be that we are watching our Lord put Peter back together again? He is giving Peter back his dignity, his self-esteem. Our Lord has an intimate knowledge of human nature. He knows that those who have faced their own weaknesses and limitations are ideally prepared to lead and care for others. Having accepted themselves, they can have a new confidence and a new sense of self-worth that makes leadership possible.

Fourth Sunday of Easter

Acts 9:36–43
Psalm 23
Revelation 7:9–17
John 10:22–30

Weavings

The theme is that of our Lord being in every sense the source of life.

First Reading. Peter, visiting in the area of Lydda, is called to Joppa, where he recalls a woman from death.

The Psalm. The timeless portrait of God as a shepherd of our souls, a shepherd for us, embodied in our Lord.

Second Reading. John shows us the hosts before the throne of God, all looking to the risen Christ — the Lamb — as the source of grace.

The Gospel. In response to questioning, our Lord says that hearing him and knowing his purpose are possible only by following him faithfully.

Reflections

First Reading

[Peter] turned to the body and said, "Tabitha, get up." In the short sharp command, we hear an echo of our Lord's words to Lazarus. *Lazarus, come out!* As we watch this event take place, we find increasing evidence that there was present, in these first months of the church's life, an extraordinary power to heal. This power extends even to the event we see here, where a woman who is considered dead by all who know her is recalled to life by the apostle Peter.

This incident is even more significant for Christians today, as we witness the phenomenal return of countless ministries of healing in today's church. In numerous congregations, the ancient rite of the laying on of hands with prayer is being practised again. As an extension of this ministry, we are seeing the proliferation of pastoral care teams, many eager to take training to carry out their new-found commitments. This development is all the more remarkable because it is happening at a time when the church is struggling desperately to remain creative and viable in a vastly changing society. It would appear that, even while religious institutions are undergoing threat and turmoil, certain gifts of the Spirit are being given again more richly than they have been experienced in times when church structures seemed strong and confident.

Calling the saints and widows, [Peter] showed her to be alive. This striking picture prompts us to form questions that apply at many levels of today's Christian community: "What level of new life have we got to show within and beyond the Christian community? Where are lives being changed? Where are healings of many kinds taking place?" And there is a question beyond these: "How can Christians come to realize that much of this work of our Lord and of the Holy Spirit remains hidden and unrealized, because of the widespread unwillingness of men and women to witness, even among friends, to what Christian faith means to them, and to the gifts they have received from it?"

The witness of one person in a congregation, given simply and quietly — perhaps offering thanks for the healing of illness or relationship, or telling the story of a newly discovered faith — can be incalculably effective in a community's life. One can picture Peter and Tabitha standing together in front of others, witnessing to the potential for resurrection in the Christian fellowship. And one can also imagine a person standing today in front of their own congregation — or chatting with others in their lives who are not of the fellowship of the faith — and by their quiet, reasonable, sincere witness, having an immensely powerful effect on the questing of others for faith.

The Psalm

The Wadi Kelt is a deep valley with precipitous sides. It runs from a point north-east of Jerusalem, cuts through the edge of the escarpment, and opens out onto the floor of the Jordan valley. Because of its depth, the valley loses the evening sun early and fills with shadows. Frequently people will point into the shadows, reminding their listeners of the verse in this psalm where the poet says, *Though I walk through the valley of the shadow of death, I shall fear no evil; for you are with me.* It is a tribute to the greatness of this psalm that centuries later people feel impelled to give the image an actual geography.

The Lord is my shepherd. In our Lord's day, shepherding was very low on the occupational scale. Shepherds did a lonely and dangerous job that needed to be done, but they paid a price. They were generally regarded as misfits, loners, on the edge of society, usually mistrusted, sometimes — perhaps because of their toughness — feared. Once again, as he has associated with tax gatherers, prostitutes, and Samaritans, Jesus identifies himself with shepherds, thus elevating their role by adding the qualities of caring and responsibility.

Commenting on this psalm is rather like commenting on the Mona Lisa or La Pieta or any other great work. The images speak for themselves across culture and time. The very language of this psalm has a healing quality. *The Lord ... makes me lie down ... leads me ... revives my soul ... guides me ... [comforts] me.* Each of these phrases responds to a deep human need. The hurt are given comfort, the weary are invited to rest, the lost are assured of guidance, the depressed are offered revival of the spirit. Every word reassures the mind and soothes the spirit.

As if these things were not enough, the psalm now offers an image of welcome and hospitality. *You are with me ... You spread a table before me ... you have anointed my head with oil ... my cup is running over.* The traveller has come home. Hope and confidence return. It is once again possible to engage life. *Surely your goodness and mercy shall follow me all the days of my life.*

Second Reading

By the time that the Book of Revelation was being written, Christians had begun to discover that their allegiance could have a high cost. Already in some parts of the empire, there were occasions of persecution. To some extent, this passage of John speaks to people who either have had loved ones become the victims of persecution, or have themselves been through some ordeal. And so the guiding angel, responding to the evangelist's question about the great host before them, says, *These are they who have come out of the great ordeal.* In these words, John is offering to people of his own time a hope in spite of suffering experienced.

After this I looked, and there was a great multitude ... from all tribes and peoples and languages, standing before the throne and before the Lamb, robed in white, with palm branches in their hands. It is easy for most of us in the developed world to forget that a passage such as this can continue to be a source of hope and comfort for many Christians who have experienced atrocious agonies throughout the world. To hear this passage after the Ruwanda-Burundi tragedy or the Croatia-Bosnia war, provides a searing reminder of the terrible realities of some Christian experience.

It is important to notice that John places the lamb at the centre of this vast tableau. The huge throng stands *before the Lamb.* The great cry that goes up tells of salvation that *belongs to our God ... and to the Lamb.* Again, the white robes have been washed *in the blood of the Lamb.* All of these images and statements are for one purpose — to emphasize the absolute centrality of our Lord in the work of salvation. Then comes the loveliest image of all, one that has been of immeasurable comfort to men and women down through the ages, especially in their times of desolation and mourning: *They will hunger no more, and thirst no more ... for the Lamb at the centre of the throne [notice again the centrality of our Lord] will be their shepherd, and he will guide them ... and God will wipe away every tear from their eyes.* Our Lord as ruler. Our Lord as shepherd. Our Lord as guide. Our Lord as comforter.

The Gospel

To be in Jerusalem in January is to recall this passage vividly. To stand at that time of year in the area where once the temple stood, and to look across to the surrounding walls where *the portico of Solomon* was, is to realize exactly why our Lord was seeking the shelter of the walkway. It was bitterly cold, as only Jerusalem can be in the winter, lying high up on the central rock spine of the country. John simply tells us *it was winter* because he too knows what the weather can be like here.

We can picture the scene. People have their outer robes gathered around them for warmth. Faces peer out from heavy cowls. The atmosphere is tense. There are a thousand questions being asked about Jesus. An answer is required — now! Jesus' reply is probably annoying and frustrating. *I have told you, and you do not believe.* Then he adds a sentence that speaks to us all. Jesus implies that it is not so much his words that point to his identity as his deeds. *The works that I do in my Father's name testify to me.* The same is true for each one of us. Our true identity is displayed much more in our actions than in our words.

Once again, Jesus says something that applies for all time. He speaks of those who follow him. *You do not believe, because you do not belong to my sheep.* He seems to be saying that our ability to hear him and believe in him grows out of our relationship with him, and this relationship in turn grows out of our commitment to follow him.

Fifth Sunday
of Easter

Acts 11:1–18
Psalm 148
Revelation 21:1–6
John 13:31–35

Weavings

In every reading there is a theme of breaking through and expanding beyond previously known boundaries.

First Reading. Peter has a dream in Joppa that tremendously expands his understanding of God's ways.

The Psalm. To try to describe the glory of God in creation, the psalmist reaches out toward every aspect of that creation.

Second Reading. John attempts to find language for nothing less than the total transformation of creation.

The Gospel. Jesus speaks of the glory hidden within himself, as well as the glory hidden in human love.

Reflections

First Reading

This passage is immediate and vivid because it sounds so human. We hear Peter trying to describe an experience that has shattered beliefs strongly held since childhood. To tell such a story is difficult, especially when no one listening to you has shared your experience and when everyone is quite determined, at least initially, to consider you out of your mind!

Peter has a lot of explaining to do. He has done something unprecedented in Jewish life. He has shared a meal with Gentile companions. How could this have happened? Voices demand an explanation when he arrives back in Jerusalem, a city where tradition runs deep and change is suspect. They ask, *Why did you go to uncircumcised men and eat with them?*

Peter does the only thing he can do. He has no reasoned argument to present, only a dream so vivid that for him it became reality. He believes that God addressed him in a dream. He describes every clearly remembered detail. How could he forget? His life is forever changed, and with it, the course of the new faith is also forever changed. This is the significance of the episode. We, as Christians today, are as we are because of this dream in long-ago Joppa.

Peter then explains what made the dream a reality. He was not even quite awake when visitors came and escorted him to a Gentile home. In front of Peter's eyes they received the Holy Spirit. Into Peter's mind came the voice of Jesus saying, *John baptized with water, but you will be baptized with the Holy Spirit.* And here it was coming true, in a Roman family and a Roman home!

There is something wonderfully immediate about Luke's account of this particular moment when Peter has finished his tale. We can almost see Peter's face and body language as he says, *If then God gave them the same gift that he gave us when we believed in the Lord Jesus Christ, who was I that I could hinder God?*

For us, moving year by year into an increasingly multi-racial and multi-cultural society, this passage is eloquent. I would suggest that it asks us to live in this society as a Christian but to remain open to the ability of the Holy Spirit to work through men and women who do not share this tradition with us. It holds a mirror to our eyes and forces us to ask the question Peter voices, "Who [am] I that I [can] hinder God?"

The Psalm

If the camera lens had been invented when this psalm was written, we would have had a magnificent video. It would have shown space shots borrowed from NASA: *Praise the Lord from the heavens.* It would have ransacked the great paintings of the Renaissance for majestic winged creatures: *Praise him, all you angels of his ... all his host.* Then we would have been hurled through the solar system — *sun and moon* — and on through the galaxy — *all you shining stars.* We would even have sailed out to the great aerial oceans that were once thought to be above the skies — "waters above the heavens."

Perhaps this is where the twentieth-century video would stop. After all, everything has been shown. But not so for the psalmist. Beyond the deepest heaven and the farthest star lies the ultimate beauty and majesty who *commanded and they were created,* the One who *gave a law which shall not pass away.*

Now we are again transported by the camera. This time we explore earth itself. We plunge into the ocean to encounter *sea-*

monsters and all deeps. We are swept through weather systems and climates — *fire and hail, snow and fog, tempestuous winds.* Once again we notice that these scenes are presented to us as more than mere phenomena of nature. They do not merely exist. They are all *doing [God's] will.*

Now we climb *mountains and all hills.* We sweep through groves of *fruit trees and all cedars.* We run with *wild beasts and all cattle,* shrink from *creeping things,* and wonder at the grace of *wingèd birds.* Suddenly we are in the human world, its structures and institutions — *princes and all rulers of the world.* Beyond them, never quite to be made prisoners of structures and authorities, are *young men and maidens, old and young together.* Finally our ears are anointed with the combined song of all creation, singing not of its own glory but of God, whose *splendour is over earth and heaven.*

With poetry like this, no wonder the ancients believed that the stars sang! Perhaps they do, and it is our ears that need opening. Perhaps we need to be *a people who are near [to God.]*

Second Reading

The more one appreciates the task that John set himself in passages such as this, the more one realizes how magnificently he has succeeded. To describe what he was envisioning — nothing less than the transformation of all creation — he has to find the most exalted language possible. And he has succeeded.

A new heaven and a new earth. In seven simple words John triggers a dream, a vision, that will attract men and women in every subsequent generation. Philosophers will search for ideas to renew society. Poets, like John himself, will sing of a wondrous vision. Theologians will propose a moral basis to transform society. Sociologists will outline ideas and systems. Dictators will mould society to their will, apparently for society's ben-

efit. Saints will sacrifice life itself, to pursue a vision of justice —
a vision that will reflect the perfection of John's image of a *holy
city.*

Yet we need to be aware of a reality we can easily miss as we
read. We need to hear the warning in the words that describe
the holy city as *coming down out of heaven from God.* In other
words, not all our hands, however willing, not all our thinking,
however brilliant, can build this city. It is a gift given *from God.*
But this does not mean that our human hands and minds and
spirits are helpless spectators to the work of God in history.
This truth is made very clear in John's next statements. *See, the
home of God is among mortals. He will dwell with them; they
will be his peoples, and God himself will be with them.* The
vision of the city of God is given to us, and we are called to
work for its fulfillment, even though we know that it will never
be perfectly fulfilled in time and history. But our human lives
achieve their deepest and richest sense of meaning when we are
consciously offering our gifts for God's purpose in society.

Perhaps we need to grasp, more than any other words in
this passage, the assurance that God is *making all things new.*
At a time such as this, when the tides of change are surging so
tumultuously around us, the attitude emerging from this text
can be a source of grace and strength. To believe truly that God
is *the beginning and the end* of all that is taking place in our
time, can be for our sometimes weary and thirsty souls *a gift
from the spring of the water of life.*

The Gospel

We are at the terrible moment when Judas has risen from the
table and slipped out of the upper room. The circle of the twelve
is broken, and the stage is set for events that will change the
world. Our Lord's emotions and thoughts must have become
extremely intense at this moment, for immediately he says, *Now*

*the Son of Man has been glorified, and God has been glorified
in him ... Little children, I am with you only a little longer.*

It is difficult for us to probe the meaning of the first part of
this statement. But I think that from it we can gather some
meaning to apply to our own lives. Because my life has been
given to me by God, it follows that, through my living, I am
able in some sense to glorify God. Much of my living may not
give glory to God. If anything, my great temptation as a human
being is to seize any available glory for myself! But sometimes,
by the grace and gift of God, I am enabled to say or do something that does give glory to God.

In my human searching for what it means to give glory to
God in my living, our Lord now offers very clear direction. Saying that it is clear does not say it is easy! Jesus says in that upper
room, *I give you a new commandment, that you love one another ... By this everyone will know that you are my disciples.*
More than in any other way, I give glory to God by my capacity
to love.

Sixth Sunday of Easter

Acts 16:9–15
Psalm 67
Revelation 21:10, 22–22:5
John 14:23–29

Weavings

Once again there is a pushing out of boundaries, a challenging of limits.

First Reading. Paul, now on the western edge of Asia, is invited in a dream to cross into Europe.

The Psalm. The psalmist's vision of God now exceeds all limitations.

Second Reading. John's vision of the Holy City becomes our ultimate hope for society.

The Gospel. Jesus tells the disciples that beyond their relationship with him is their relationship with the Holy Spirit.

Reflections

First Reading

We are watching a man tossing and turning in sleep. If we bend over him, we can probably see his eyes moving rapidly under closed eyelids. He is dreaming. This is one of the most important dreams a human being will ever have, because it will change the course of Western civilization. We are watching Paul as he lies asleep on the western edge of Asia in the port city of Troas.

For all we know, Paul may have spent the previous evening pacing on the beach near the city. If he did, he would have seen the sunset across the Aegean Sea and, perhaps, wondered about the world that lay across the water. Over there was the edge of Europe. And this is very significant for us, because this dream of Paul will bring the gospel of Jesus Christ across those gold-flecked waters to the Europe that eventually will take it to the rest of the world.

In his dream, Paul is confronted by a man who makes a simple but moving appeal. *Come over to Macedonia and help us.* Paul's response is typical: *Immediately ... we set sail.* What follows is history. Paul and his two companions, Silas and perhaps Luke (the narrative begins to speak of "we" here), go to a public gathering place. There they engage in conversation with a woman who is a Gentile but has begun to worship the God of Israel. Her name is Lydia. Eventually the travellers stay in her house. The meeting is immensely significant. From it will come one of the most flourishing Christian communities that Paul ever founded, a community to which he later writes one of his happiest letters.

In this passage, we are once again hearing the theme of these post-Easter Sundays. Boundary after boundary is being crossed in the name of the risen Lord. The implication already is that there are no limits, as indeed there are not even to our own day. There are parts of the world where Christian faith is spreading widely in many forms. It is very important for us in the West to realize this, as we struggle with the relevance of Christian faith in our own societies.

The Psalm

There is a line in this psalm that probably indicates the season when it was first sung. *The earth has brought forth her increase.* It could have been harvest time. This is the loveliest time in Israel — for that matter, the loveliest in any land — when the yearly cycle brings forth again the fruits of the earth. The people are gathered in the temple, and they are thanking God for blessings once again received. They are asking that God, who has given the harvest, will also bless them in other ways. *May God, our own God, give us his blessing.* As we use the psalm in this post-Easter season, we can treat it as a thanksgiving for our Lord's resurrection. In harvesting terms, death was sown, life was reaped.

Notice how these people regard God — God is *our own God.* One might think that such language would restrict their thinking, and therefore limit their prayer life to their own concerns as a people. But the very opposite is true. Certainly they bring the concerns of Israel before God, but they never stop there. And this openness is so important. We need to hear it in this psalm and in other psalms. Referring to God as "our own God" never deludes Israel into thinking that God is limited to them. They believe passionately that they are the concern of God, but they do not think they are God's only concern.

May God be merciful to us and bless us. So begins the song. But it takes only a moment to hurl us out among the nations. *Let your ways be known on earth, your saving health among all nations ... Let the peoples praise you ... Let the nations be glad.*

Now comes a statement made so casually that we can easily miss the huge claim it is making: *You [God] guide all the nations upon earth.* The people of Israel cannot conceive of God as being less than universal. Perhaps we need to ask ourselves if our concept of God is as large and as inclusive as that of the people who gave us this psalm.

Second Reading

We are once again sharing John's great vision of the Holy City. As he points to various aspects of the city, he is teaching his listeners some important truths about the life of the Christian community and human society in general.

I saw no temple in the city, for its temple is the Lord God the Almighty and the Lamb. As I read this, I think I am being given a kind of warning about the institutional church. It is not an absolute. It is a flawed instrument through which the will of God is served — alas, sometimes not served — in time and history. This is not to say for a moment that the church can be dismissed as unnecessary or irrelevant. To appreciate this truth, we have only to follow John's gaze toward the throne of God in his vision. Beside that throne stands the risen Lord, *the Lamb,* and the central truth about our Lord is that he submitted to becoming a prisoner of human flesh, even to dying as a human being, so that the church might be given birth. We can go even further if we are prepared to take the images of John's vision seriously. He has told us of the seven spirits of God around the throne. These are images of the Holy Spirit that gave the church its birth at Pentecost.

The glory of God is [the city's] light, and its lamp is the Lamb. John is saying to us that the source of any society's overall health is the glory — or the will and grace and power — of God. He is also saying that a society prepared to accept Christ as the Lord of life has found a light to live by. To the degree that any society measures itself by these criteria, it will be strong

and secure. It will also have standards and values that other societies will seek out: *The nations will walk by its light.* A society
that acknowledges God as the source of life will have a resource
for keeping its life clean and pure: *The river of the water of life
... flowing from the throne of God ... through ... the city.*

We can dismiss such envisioning of perfection as nothing
more than dreaming. Yet the power of this vision has called men
and women in every generation to work for the well-being of
the society they live in. We are not to see the perfection of the
Holy City within history, but to work for it in history gives human life meaning and purpose.

The Gospel

*Jesus answered him, "Those who love me will keep my word,
and my Father will love them, and we will come and make our
home with them."* At first impression, it is easy to assume that
these statements of our Lord are gentle and soothing. After all,
the word "love" occurs again and again. Yet when we listen carefully, we realize that this love is what we sometimes call "tough
love." *Those who love me will keep my word.* We are being
told that the proof of love is the extent to which it issues in
behaviour. In these statements, our Lord gives the word "love"
a very different meaning from that generally understood in the
Western world today. In our culture, love is a feeling, a passion,
an experience that happens to us and to which we respond — or
perhaps do not respond. There is certainly feeling in our response to our Lord, but he demands that our feelings also become actions.

*We will come to them [who keep my word] and make our
home with them.* Our Lord seems to be saying that faith in him
— if it be sustained and genuine and grounded in action —
becomes a relationship with him.

I have said these things to you while I am still with you. But the Advocate, the Holy Spirit, whom the Father will send in my name, will teach you everything. Once again we are reminded of the nature of Christian faith. It is a process in which we are always being called to further maturity. In so far as it is a relationship with God, it is always changing. The present focus for the disciples is Jesus. From him they draw insight and direction. But this cannot last forever. In fact, it is about to be withdrawn. Another focus will have to be found. Their new focus will be the Holy Spirit. Unlike Jesus, who is other than themselves, the Holy Spirit will be found inside themselves. Reliance on an exterior source is about to end. Reliance on an interior source is about to begin.

Jesus offers a paradox. *I am going away, and I am coming to you.* If we are prepared to think about it, this is the recurring pattern of our faith journey. There is always the coming of a source of grace, and then the going away of this source. If the source of grace is a soul friend, a circle of support, a congregation, a priest, there will come a time of change. We move away or someone else does. Someone dies. Something changes. But if we remain open to this constant process, it is also true that someone or something comes, and again we receive grace. True, the old has not been reproduced, but a new grace has been given.

Seventh Sunday of Easter

Acts 16:16–34
Psalm 97
Revelation 22:12–14, 16–17, 20–21
John 17:20–26

Weavings

In all these readings there is a strong call to commitment and self giving.

First Reading. Paul and Silas show total commitment to their Lord and to the missionary task they have embraced.

The Psalm. For the psalmist, the only possible relationship with God is one of absolute submission.

Second Reading. Jesus, as the Lord who has given himself to experience human life, asks us to regard him as the beginning and end of our lives.

The Gospel. Our Lord has shown to his disciples the love of the Father. His prayer is that their lives may reflect that love in response.

Reflections

First Reading

A continuing theme throughout the readings in this post-Easter season is the certainty that nothing can stop the spread of the new faith. It is easy to gloss over the severity of the obstacles that had to be overcome, not to mention the threats that faced these early travellers for Christianity. This passage clearly shows what Paul and his friends were up against.

This story communicates the extraordinary enthusiasm and commitment of that first generation of believers. It shows the almost unbelievable risks they were prepared to take, and the physical suffering they were prepared to endure. The contrast to most contemporary Christian commitment is salutary, to say the least!

Paul and Silas — and perhaps Luke — are in Philippi. In all these cities, life is intense and volatile. In these streets, Paul and Silas are strangers. To make things more dangerous, they are also Jews, always in danger of becoming the focus of antagonism.

A young woman, owned by people we would probably call pimps, follows the strangers. She has probably overheard them speaking in some nearby public place. Her wild shouting calls attention to them. Paul loses patience and confronts her. Somehow he succeeds in steadying the young woman. He speaks the name of Jesus. It is highly unlikely that, at this early stage of the faith, the young woman would have known of our Lord, unless she had overheard Paul mention him. But Paul's way of confronting her pierces whatever has enslaved the young woman. She is no longer of use to her owners.

All hell breaks loose! By one stroke, a lucrative enterprise has been ruined. In an orgy of self-righteous protesting, the girl's owners haul the visitors into court. As we listen to the charges, we can hear the moral posturing: *These men are disturbing our city; they are Jews and are advocating customs that are not lawful for us as Romans to adopt or observe.* What noble citizens these pimps are! One can almost see the poses of innocence and affronted loyal citizenship.

What follows is very grim indeed. The travellers are stripped naked and publicly flogged. Apart from the shame, a public flogging is extremely painful, and can be fatal. As if this is not enough, the travellers are flung into what Luke calls *the innermost cell* and, as well, are fastened into stocks.

We need to realize the extreme danger that Paul and Silas have landed in. Only then can we realize what it means when we hear them, as did their fellow prisoners, *praying and singing hymns to God.* Luke actually adds the vivid detail, *the prisoners were listening to them.*

Then comes the earthquake. Such tremors are still frequent in this part of the world. The jail, probably primitive, is in a shambles. This is the guard's worst nightmare. If the prisoners escape, not only his job will be on the line, but his life as well. To his utter astonishment, one of these strangers takes complete control of the situation, through a kind of natural authority. The jailor may have been a former military man, able to recognize authority. And so, he now behaves instinctively. He throws himself before Paul and says something very human: *Sirs, what must I do to be saved?*

What various spiritual meanings have been heaped on this desperate cry for help! We can be sure that this terrified man had little thought of things religious! His mind was on such concrete things as seeing the sun come up in the morning, and returning to his home in the evening alive! But this does not mean that his cry cannot take on great significance. Brilliantly, Paul uses this instinctive cry for help as an opportunity to give meaning and direction to this man's life, beyond his wildest imaginations. Paul not only saves his life, but offers him a new way of life in Christ.

How can we interpret such moments for today? A friend asks us for help or advice. We give it as best we can. But how often do we take a chance on mentioning, in some simple acceptable way, how much Christian faith or the Christian community means in our own lives, offering these things as a possibility in our friend's life? We very badly need to develop this ability — we could almost call it an art. These are the simple and natural ways in which this elusive and often frightening thing we call evangelism can be done.

The Psalm

There is much in the psalms to keep the environmentalist happy. Again and again nature is pointed out as the domain of God. Seas, mountains, rivers, forests — all are sacred. Among them and through them God moves. But it is easy to miss something essential in these images of God. Often in the world of environmental concerns, the earth is considered sacred. The insight that the planet may be a self-regulating organism — the Gaia hypothesis — can sometimes lead to our regarding the earth as a kind of god.

In the psalms, we hear a strong corrective to this. We have it here. The first images are very physical and external. *Let the earth rejoice ... let the multitude of the isles be glad. Clouds and darkness are round about him ... fire goes before him ... His lightnings light up the world.* Nature is to God as it were a garment. Clouds and darkness are around God. Fire goes before God. It is God's lightnings that light the world. Why does the earth rejoice? Because *the Lord is King!* Nature is not the ultimate domain of the sacred. Nature partakes of the sacredness of which God is the source.

But we have not yet fully expressed the depth of this and other psalms. The psalmist goes beyond and through nature. Important as it is to see God as the creator of nature, it is even more important to probe the nature of this creating God. The psalmist frequently makes these probings, but always arrives at the same emphasis. In this psalm, we are told that *righteousness and justice are the foundations of his throne*. The people of God rejoice in the fact that God is a God of justice. The great gift of this conviction is its unshakable hope. Because God is essentially and eternally just, then justice will eventually triumph, no matter how awful present circumstances may be. *The heavens declare his righteousness,* says the psalmist. The conviction that justice cannot finally be defeated has upheld many through desperately dark times.

Second Reading

For the last few weeks, we have been moving through some passages of this book of John. By sharing in the magnificent visions that John gives us, we are probing to the end of time and anticipating the consequences of our Lord's resurrection. When we do this, we arrive in a city. It is no ordinary city. It is a Holy City, under the sovereignty of God. *Shalom* reigns.

We know that we can never build this Holy City within time and history. It remains a vision. But the power of the vision is in the energy and dedication it inspires in some men and women of every generation, as they glimpse the possibilities of a society where peace and justice reign.

In this passage, the vision of John reaches even beyond the city of God. Because we cannot bring about this Holy City ourselves, it must be brought into being from beyond us. The city comes from God.

Some sneer at such Christian belief, saying that, because this city of God cannot be found in history, it encourages Christians to regard the human struggle with too much detachment. The reality is very different. John's vision of the end or consummation of the whole of creation is one that includes the domain of time and history. Because God is creator of all, then all things lie within the domain of God. John decides to end his book with the words that he imagines emanating from our Lord: *Surely I am coming soon.* Here he expresses his conviction that, when creation is brought to consummation by God, the face and nature of that God will reflect what we saw and knew in Jesus Christ our Lord.

The Gospel

The moment is intense; the language, deeply moving. We are overhearing our Lord at prayer. The prayer is for his disciples as they move into a future that lies beyond his physical presence with them. This prayer was first said in the shadows of the upper room the night before he was crucified. We are hearing it now as they would often remember it in the years that followed.

At an earlier stage in his gospel, John tells us that Jesus *knew what was in everyone* (John 2:25). This prayer suggests that our Lord fully understood, and was most concerned about, the human propensity for disunity! How right our Lord was! Again and again we hear him pray, *that they may all be one ... that the world may know.* As we know to our great sorrow, we have been anything but one, and the world has thereby greatly disbelieved!

On this Sunday, we are in the last hours of the Easter season. All of these Sundays have in some sense been looking back to that mysterious and massive event, trying to probe its endless meanings for us, as followers of this person who rose from the dead. This morning, our Lord seems to be telling us why it all happened.

First, it happened so that we might be *in* God, as our Lord expresses it, *As you, Father, are in me and I am in you, may they also be in us.* This sounds like such simple language, yet it speaks of something inexpressibly profound. To be *in God.* What would that mean for me? For you? Does it in any way describe the relationship we have at present with God?

The second thing our Lord prays for on our behalf is *glory.* Again, we hear his words: *Father, I desire that those ... may be with me where I am, to see my glory.* Again we have to probe for meaning, indeed, for many levels of meaning. How can you and I ever see the glory of our Lord? In an effort to reply, I recall the experience of the three disciples on the mountain of transfiguration. They saw our Lord's glory. Very simply, this tells me that I have to commit time and effort to my relationship with him. There has to be what I will call some "climbing," some determination to set aside times and put myself in certain places — perhaps of beauty or quietness or solitude — if I am to catch glimpses of the glory of being Christian.

There are very different places of glory. In fact, there is no place and no circumstance where the glory of Christ cannot be present. I will always remember Harry Williams, a monk of Mirfield, telling about being in a railway carriage in France. With him were a farmer and his young son. Suddenly the young son was torn with a seizure. Williams says that, as long as he lives, he will never forget the calm tenderness with which the father cared for his child. For Williams, at that moment, the carriage was filled with glory.

I am sure that my relating this story will release many hearing it to recall moments of glory in nature, in worship, in relationships, in suffering, in ecstatic joy, in almost every aspect of life, when we became aware that our Lord himself, risen and glorious, was mysteriously present in the moment.

The third reason that the glory of Easter took place is so that our lives will be characterized, more than anything else, by the gift to love and be loved. Our Lord prays, *I made your name known to them, and I will make it known, so that the love with which you have loved me may be in them, and I in them.* We have only to read these words and we bow our heads in silence and shame. We know that we have failed to love. And so we always remember this failure when we kneel in general confession: "We have not loved you with our whole heart. We have not loved our neighbours as ourselves." Here there can be no self-justification, no pretense, no well-intentioned assurances of self-improvement. There is room for only one thing here — one thing we are helpless to provide for ourselves, one thing the risen Christ must give if we are to find peace. We seek forgiveness.

Perhaps in forgiveness, more than in anything else, we find the most profound level of the reason for Good Friday and Easter. As Mrs. Alexander wrote in her deceptively simple yet most profound hymn, *"He died that we might be forgiven."*

Day of Pentecost

Acts 2:1–21
Psalm 104:24–34, 35b
Romans 8:14–17
John 14:8–17 (25–27)

Weavings

There is no need to search for a theme in today's readings!
Every reading tells us of the work of the Holy Spirit.

First Reading. We are present when the embryonic Christian community is filled with the Spirit.

The Psalm. The song identifies the Spirit of God as the instrument through whom creation comes into being.

Second Reading. To be Christian is to have received the Spirit of God into oneself. It is also to be called to a life of service by this same Spirit.

The Gospel. As Jesus himself has been a bridge between God and his disciples, so he now offers the Spirit as the go-between.

Note

When we come to preach or study or meditate on the readings for this Sunday — and also next Sunday (Pentecost) — we stand surrounded by a great mystery, that of the Holy Spirit of God. How can we possibly access the meaning and understand the implications of this event? My own instinct is not to attempt explanation, but to let the narrative work its wonder and evoke its own response. This is the method of Luke and Paul and John. Not one of them philosophizes, analyzes, or explains. Each simply tells us about something that happened to change him and other people forever.

Reflections

First Reading

We are somewhere in Jerusalem in a large room filled with people. What brings them here is the one thing they have in common. It is still only weeks since they were shaken to the core by the news that Jesus, whom some of them had seen die, is among them. Since that time, many of them have experienced his presence in ways that they find difficult to put into language. But they are all absolutely agreed that the presence is a reality — not dreamed, not imagined, not a wish fulfillment — a reality.

The atmosphere in the room is electric with excitement. Anyone of them if asked would probably not have been able to give a reason. But there is at this moment an intense excitement.

Even as we ask, there is a change in the atmosphere. Perhaps all sound dropped away into silence. Then it happened. Some years later a doctor in Antioch will try to bring us into that moment. His name is Luke. Even he gropes for words, but they are magnificent words, and they will speak to Christians until the end of time. *Suddenly from heaven there came a sound like the rush of a violent wind, and it filled the entire house where they were sitting. Divided tongues, as of fire, appeared among them, and a tongue rested on each of them.*

We can approach no nearer than this. All the curious questions such as "How? Why? What did it mean? What was really happening?" are of no avail. All we know is the effect on those people. *All of them were filled with the Holy Spirit.* Again our questions tumble out: "What does it mean to be filled with the Holy Spirit? Is this normal? Is this something long ago that happened at the dawn of the Christian movement but could never be part of our experience?" As our questions resound, Luke continues, *All of them ... began to speak in other languages, as the Spirit gave them ability ... the crowd gathered and was bewildered ... They asked, "Are not all these who are speaking Galileans? How is it we hear, each of us, in our own native language?"*

How indeed! We will never know. There are differing reactions in the surrounding crowd. Some hear their own language; others dismiss the events as a drunken outburst. At the height of the commotion, Peter rises to speak. He has no doubts about what has happened. Since he and every Jew within earshot was a child, they have been taught that God has promised, *I will pour out my Spirit upon all flesh.* We do know that something extraordinarily powerful happened and was never forgotten. The effect on the early small community was to energize and inspire them beyond description.

How do you prove the reality of all this? Very simply. You get a mirror and look at your own face, or you look at the faces in a circle of Bible study or prayer or healing of which you may be a member, or you look at those who walk forward with you to receive eucharist. You and these others are proof that something extraordinary happened on that long-ago day. A people was brought into existence — a people of God, a people of our Lord Jesus Christ. Since that day, this people has existed, grown, changed, struggled, prayed, worshipped. One day you became a member of this people, this body, by baptism. You and they are the proof. Now each of you must ask what the quality of this proof is.

There is another way to seek proof for this event. Ever since then, at different times in the long story of this people, and in various places, and with different levels of intensity, men and women have experienced what was experienced in that room. They have felt themselves to be filled with God's Holy Spirit. The encounter has manifested in countless different ways — some quietly serene, some wildly tempestuous and disturbing; some in an moment of sacrament, some in a moment of scripture study; and let us never forget, some in the most unlikely and unexpected places and times.

And so I say to you what Peter said to the surrounding crowd on that day, *Let this be known to you and listen to what I say. Indeed, these are not drunk ... No, this is what was spoken through the prophet Joel ... "I will pour out my Spirit upon all flesh."*

The Psalm

I am about nine years of age. It is Wednesday afternoon choir practice. Through the half-open window, I can see the green of the woods opposite the church. Outside is freedom and play. But suddenly I hear verses of this psalm, and I am transported to a grand different scene. Our piping soprano voices sing, "There go the ships; and there is Leviathan, whom thou has formed to take his pastime therein."

Yes, these are the words I would have sung that day. I was being captured by the language of Miles Coverdale, writing to me from the sixteenth century, telling me of *the great and wide sea, with its living things too many to number, creatures both small and great.* Slightly different language from that of today, but the same images come cascading into my mind. There is the thunder of the ocean, and the booming call of some vast form rising and falling in the waves just beyond the prow of my imaginary ship.

I am using memory to point out the majesty and grand vision of this psalm. To give me images of the work of the creating spirit of God, the psalmist is deliberately thinking in great landscapes and endless vistas. For him God is one who is *[wrapped in] light as with a cloak.* For him God is one who *[makes] the clouds your chariot* and *the winds your messengers.* Paraded before us is the whole vast canvas of creation: *the waters ... the mountains ... the springs ... the beasts of the field ... the birds of the air.* This is a God who makes wine — oceans of it! A God who makes bread — mountains of it! By the power of this God, rises the glory of the sun. And under its golden light, there walks another creature fashioned by God: *People go out to their work and to their labour until the evening.*

Whether one is child or adult, this wonderful song gives us a vision of the creating Spirit of God. *When you send forth your Spirit ... they are created.* Yet vast and wonderful and beautiful though this creation be, when *you [God] hide your face ... they are terrified. When you take away their breath ... they die and return to their dust.* All this God has to do is *touch the mountains and they smoke — look on the earth and it trembles.*

No wonder the psalmist intends to *praise my God while I have being.* A terrifying thought for a choirboy, Leviathan notwithstanding!

Second Reading

For all who are led by the Spirit of God are children of God. Paul is trying to hammer home into the minds of his time that, when one becomes a Christian, one has been called into a relationship. Not only into a relationship, but into a loving relationship. For Paul, this is of paramount importance.

Not ... a spirit of slavery ... but ... a spirit of adoption. Paul knew that he was writing to many who had come out of religious systems where fear was dominant — fear of a hostile pagan god, or fear of not carrying out the demands of a legal system. Perhaps we need to remind ourselves that such things are by no means in the past. Many people's Christian faith can be tinged with disturbing fears arising from childhood traumas, or with apprehensions of a God whose laws, if broken, bring punishment.

When we cry, "Abba! Father!" it is that very Spirit bearing witness with our spirit that we are children of God. We instinctively want to turn to God as a parent figure. This inherent desire is an indication that within us already there is a flame of God's Spirit that calls us back to the source of the love we long for.

If children, then heirs. When we become Christian, we enter into an inheritance. Between our humanity and the being of God, there is a vast gulf. But that gulf is continually being bridged by our Lord Jesus Christ, who lived our humanity with such perfection that in him the gulf closes. If I become Christian, I inherit "the way back to God" through Jesus as my Lord. The way back is not without cost. It involves subordinating my will to that of another. But there is glory in this cost. For I find that the will to whom I surrender gives back to me my own will transformed.

The Gospel

The scene is the upper room. The disciples are sitting around the table. They have been here for some time. The night is long. The atmosphere is tense. Everyone knows that this is no ordinary occasion. There is a sense that something terrible is going to happen, but no one knows what it is. There is a suspicion that time is running out, that if things remain to be said, they had better be said. If questions remain — and there are many — they had better be asked.

Philip breaks the silence: *Lord, show us the Father, and we will be satisfied.* There is a kind of desperation in his question, as if Philip suddenly realizes that he knows almost nothing about that which is more than can possibly be imagined. Philip wants to know everything in one clarifying moment, so that he can understand why his life has been turned upside down by this friend across the shadowed room. We all have known occasions like this, when the mystery of life is too great, and we do not understand, and we want to be told something simple and reassuring, because we are lonely or sad or frightened.

The response Philip receives — and presumably the others overhear — shows that Jesus understands his friend's feeling. The response is gentle and reassuring and patient, and it ends with a promised gift.

Jesus says three things to his friends. First, he tells them that in him they see the face of ultimate reality, and he reassures them that this reality is loving and creative. *Believe me that I am in the Father and the Father is in me.*

The second thing Jesus says is that the person who believes in him has a vocation to serve in the world in the same way that Jesus has served in the world. *The one who believes in me will also do the works that I do.*

The third thing Jesus says is that those who believe in him and offer themselves in his service will discover in themselves a Spirit whom they will recognize as his Spirit. *I will ask the Father, and he will give you another Advocate ... the Spirit of truth ... You know him, because he abides with you, and he will be in you.*

Trinity Sunday

Proverbs 8:1–4, 22–31
Psalm 8
Romans 5:1–5
John 16:12–15

Weavings

As with last Sunday our theme is very clear in all First Read-
ings. We are being given a succession of images and events by
which we can approach the mystery of the being of God.

First Reading. The writer takes us to the morning of the
universe and shows us Wisdom, the companion of God in the
work of creation.

The Psalm. The psalmist stretches language to the utmost
to try to capture the awe of creation and the place of our humanity within it.

Second Reading. Paul shows that the relationship between
our Lord and ourselves can bring wholeness, peace, and grace
to us.

The Gospel. Our Lord promises his disciples that, though
the present relationship between them must end, there will be
another relationship given to them through the Holy Spirit.

Note

It is worthwhile taking note of the shortness of the readings for this Sunday. This suggests something we need to acknowledge. We are once again surrounded by a mystery. We do not need to apologize for the word "mystery." There was a time when the Christian faith was called a Mysterion. It is a lovely and rather majestic word that does justice to what we are dealing with.

When preaching or meditating on these readings, it may be best to avoid getting involved in theological conundrums, and instead approach the content simply. What do the readings say? How do we respond to what they say? We might begin by noting that the four pieces of scripture assigned for this day attempt the impossible! They try to tell us about the nature of the mystery we call God. In doing so, they conceive of a single reality that is not only unimaginably alive and varied, but is also the source of the unimaginable variety of all that exists.

Reflections

First Reading

We see the figure of a beautiful woman. She appears in many places: *On the heights, beside the way, at the crossroads.* In other words, we encounter her everywhere and in every aspect of creation. Her name is Wisdom.

Wisdom is within us and around us and in all things, because she is the companion of God the creator. We see her being formed by God before anything else: *I was set up, at the first, before the beginning of the earth.* The writer gives us a magnificent poem of the creative acts of God: *established the heavens ... drew a circle on the face of the deep ... made firm the skies ... the fountains of the deep ... assigned the sea its limit ... marked out the foundations of the earth.* In all the mighty work of creation, we see Wisdom standing beside God and acting, according to scripture, *like a master worker.* As we know, the purpose of a master worker is to carry out the plans of a designer. And so Wisdom is the means, the intermediary, by which creation takes place.

Now something totally unexpected is added, something also very beautiful. *I was daily his delight, rejoicing before him always, rejoicing in his inhabited world and delighting in the human race.* We are being told that the awe and wonder of the created universe emerges out of a relationship of mutual delight. This is extremely important because it brings us to a relationship, and relationship lies at the heart of what we believe about the mystery we call God.

The Psalm

J.B. Phillips, one of the gifted Bible translators of this century, used to insist that our God is too small! Not so for the psalmist. Millennia before NASA space exploration, he conveyed a sense of sublime infinity when he spoke of God. This is no God of a single city or nation. This is a God whose very name is *exalted ... in all the world.*

The psalmist is experiencing one of those moments that comes to us all. It may have come first to us as a child in summer camp or at a cottage or on a farm. We gaze at the night sky — the stars blazing as they never do for us in the city — with unalloyed innocence and wonder. Perhaps just such a childhood memory prompts the psalmist to acknowledge the startling wisdom that often comes *out of the mouths of infants and children.*

When I consider your heavens, the work of your fingers. What a subtle and gracefully paid compliment to the majesty of God. To send the moon and the stars on their heavenly courses requires nothing more than a flick of the divine fingers! No struggle, no challenge — a mere gesture and it is done.

Then comes a question that occurs to many of us as we gaze at the canopy of the night sky. What is my place in all of this? *What [are human beings] that you [are] mindful of [them,] mortals that you should care for them?* The question applies initially to oneself as an individual, but then it extends to encompass the whole of humanity and the mysterious human story. The psalmist is intrigued by an issue that for us has become a serious challenge: *You have given them dominion over the works of your hands.* Notice the reminder that humanity is not the maker, but merely the recipient of a gift. And what is the nature of this *dominion* that we have so sadly mismanaged and even betrayed? Even as we ask, the psalmist spells out our eternal responsibility. It is to care for *all sheep and oxen, even the wild beasts of the field, the birds of the air, [and] the fish of the sea.*

The psalmist repeatedly names God as sovereign, reminding us of our position with respect to the planetary creation. We must see ourselves as the creatures of a God who is sovereign over us and who demands us to be accountable for the gift given to us.

Second Reading

I ask myself, what does Christianity mean when it says to us that we have been "justified by faith"? Many Christian people might admit that this question never occurs to them. It is religious language that is not part of their everyday thinking. Nonetheless, the question is important, because it concerns the essential meaning of our lives.

As a human being, I am constantly aware that I am incomplete, that there is always more, that my highest attaining falls short of a mysterious something that seems to call me. I find myself dissatisfied with who and what I am. Sometimes I am even disgusted at myself. As C.S. Lewis was fond of saying, I feel exiled from a land or state of being that is somehow my natural home. In a word, I can never accept myself fully. I cannot (in the language of scripture) justify myself in my own eyes.

To all of this, Christian faith makes — if you will — an offer. It tells me that this humanity, with which I wrestle, has been lived out by One who knows intimately all the heights of fulfillment and depths of desperation that human life can bring. Because it shows me how Jesus Christ has gone before, it tells me that God understands. It offers me *peace with God,* and therefore with myself, *through our Lord Jesus Christ.* It promises that I will find new energy, *grace,* in my life, and that I will discovery flashes of *glory* in my human condition, because I will be aware that human life and all creation can reflect the glory of God.

At this stage in this short passage, we are once again shown the realism and the down-to-earthiness of Christian faith. *Suffering produces endurance, and endurance produces character, and character produces hope.* Christian faith does not come with a guarantee that there will be nothing to endure. But it does come with a promise that there will be a grace given *through the Holy Spirit that has been given to us.* Notice that scripture does not say "might be given" or "will be given if we are good enough to deserve it." It says, *has been given to us.*

The Gospel

We are again in that upper room where so much happened, and so much was said, and so much was given to us that constitutes the bedrock of our Christian faith. We enter the room through this scripture, just at the moment when our Lord is making a promise.

As with any relationship, any life lived — our own included — Jesus has found that there is not time to say everything. Even his relationship with the disciples must come to an end with things left unsaid. We might remember this when we are trying to help someone deal with a close relationship that has ended with things unsaid and unresolved. It was so with our Lord himself.

I still have many things to say to you, but you cannot bear them now. Those are his words, spoken no doubt with sadness and great seriousness. But then he makes a promise. The journey is not ended, but they will not have to continue alone. There will be another guide. *When the Spirit of truth comes, he will guide you into all the truth.*

[The Spirit] will take what is mine and declare it to you. Over the last few years, they have come to know that this voice and face across the table is their source of truth. Now they must find truth within themselves, not merely individually but also corporately, in their ongoing relationships and in their life in community.

The moment we use language like this, we know that what was said in that room, what was promised in that moment, was not said and promised merely to that long-ago group. As we listen to this scripture, we are experiencing an eternal relationship that binds the spirit within us to the Spirit of our Lord.